# NATURE SPOTTER

## Plants and Animals of Britain and Northern Europe

T0333187

**CONSULTANT: DEREK HARVEY**

**Project art editors** Polly Appleton, Kanika Kalra
**Project editor** Robin Moul
**Senior editor** Roohi Sehgal
**Additional editing** Radhika Haswani,
Gunjan Mewati, Lizzie Munsey,
Clare Lloyd, Dawn Sirett
**Additional design** Devika Awasthi, Bharti Karakoti,
Bhagyashree Nayak, Roohi Rais, Rashika Kachroo (Jacket)
**Jacket designer** Polly Appleton
**Jacket coordinator** Issy Walsh
**Project picture researcher** Sakshi Saluja
**Senior production editor** Robert Dunn
**Producer** Basia Ossowska
**DTP designers** Dheeraj Singh, Syed Md Farhan,
Vikram Singh, Ashok Kumar
**Managing editors** Monica Saigal, Penny Smith
**Managing art editors** Mabel Chan, Ivy Sengupta
**Delhi creative heads** Glenda Fernandes, Malavika Talukder
**Creative director** Helen Senior
**Publishing director** Sarah Larter

**Illustrator** Abby Cook
**Subject consultant** Derek Harvey
**Contributors** Stephanie Farrow,
Andrea Mills, Francesco Piscitelli

First published in Great Britain in 2021 by
Dorling Kindersley Limited
One Embassy Gardens, 8 Viaduct Gardens,
London, SW11 7BW

A CIP catalogue record for this book
is available from the British Library.
ISBN: 978-0-2415-0455-0

Printed and bound in China

For the curious
www.dk.com

MIX
Paper from
responsible sources
FSC
www.fsc.org   FSC™ C018179

This book was made with Forest
Stewardship Council™ certified paper –
one small step in DK's commitment to
a sustainable future. For more information
go to www.dk.com/our-green-pledge

# CONTENTS

WRITTEN BY: STEPHANIE FARROW,
ANDREA MILLS, AND FRANCESCO PISCITELLI

# HOW DO I BEGIN?

Nature is all around us, all the time. This is true whether you're on the coast, in the forest, or in a town. You'll discover all kinds of wildlife when you step outside and start exploring. Welcome to the great outdoors!

## Respecting nature

Always take care when you're out and about. Don't get too close to or disturb the animals. Avoid picking flowers or breaking branches from trees. Keep an eye out for any signs and make sure you follow their advice.

IT'S ESPECIALLY IMPORTANT NOT TO GET TOO CLOSE TO PROTECTIVE MOTHERS, LIKE THIS EIDER DUCK WITH HER EGGS.

## How to use this book

This guide introduces you to different habitats in northern Europe, showing some of the plants and animals that live in each one. It has tips on when and where to spot different species, and fascinating facts about their lives.

THE CHAPTER INTRODUCTION DESCRIBES THE ENVIRONMENT.

## HABITATS

The book is divided into six main habitats from northern Europe. Each one contains some smaller habitats, too.

## Take care

Here are some important safety tips for young nature spotters:

- Watch animals from a safe distance.
- Avoid steep cliffs and deep water.
- Wear the right clothes and bring equipment, such as a torch and map.
- Never go out alone. Always go with an adult.

ALWAYS TAKE AN ADULT. YOU CAN ALSO INVITE FRIENDS ON YOUR ADVENTURES.

THE SCENE SETTER TELLS YOU ABOUT THE HABITAT.

FULL OF STORIES ABOUT WILDLIFE

THESE PROFILES ARE FULL OF FACTS AND SPOTTING TIPS.

ACTIVITY BOXES GIVE YOU IDEAS FOR NEW THINGS TO TRY.

PICTURES SHOW YOU WHICH SPECIES TO LOOK FOR.

BRITAIN AND
NORTHERN EUROPE

## Where in the world?

The countries in Britain and northern Europe are home to a wide range of habitats. You may have to travel to different countries to visit them all, because not every country has icy tundra or sandy dunes.

**IN THE TOWN**
Towns and cities are surprisingly rich in wildlife. Scavengers live off leftover food, and buildings act like treetops for birds.

# WHERE DO I GO?

The world is made up of all sorts of environments. Plants and animals live almost everywhere in the world. You'll be able to spot something wherever you go!

**IN THE FIELDS**
The open countryside of the grassland has thick grass, hedgerows, and fields of wild flowers that all offer food and shelter.

## Habitats

These habitats are places where animals and plants live. Each habitat offers different kinds of food and shelter to wildlife, so they all have a different community of plants and animals living there.

## BY THE WATER
Water in freshwater habitats is not salty, like the sea is, so it is home to different water-loving flora and fauna.

## ON THE COAST
Our coastlines offer lots of different habitats, from craggy cliffs and stormy seas to sheltered rock pools and sandy dunes.

## ON HIGH GROUND
Craggy peaks, steep slopes, and extreme weather mean that only the toughest species can survive in the mountains.

## IN THE FOREST
The forest has lots of fruit and nuts to eat. Treetops, fallen logs, and leafy piles are ideal places to set up home in safety.

# WHEN SHOULD I GO?

One of the best things about nature spotting is you can do it at any time of day, in any kind of weather, and any day of the year. All these things play a part in exactly what wildlife you will see, so nature spotters are always busy!

### RAIN OR SHINE
Some animals, like butterflies, are easier to spot in dry weather. But others such as frogs, slugs, and snails prefer rainy days.

### DAY AND NIGHT
Most creatures are easier to spot in daylight when they are awake and active. However, some creatures come out at night, so you'll have to stay up late to see them.

## Ever-changing nature
You'll spot different things depending on when you go out. Changes in the season, time of day, temperature, tides, or weather all affect which creatures will come out.

# All year round

The changing seasons affect how animals behave, and sometimes even where they live. Many animals have set times in the year when they breed or travel to warmer areas. This means some animals are easier to spot in certain seasons.

HUNGRY BUTTERFLIES FEAST ON THE SWEET NECTAR INSIDE WILD FLOWERS IN SUMMER.

FLOWERS FILL FIELDS AND MEADOWS WITH BRIGHT COLOUR IN THE SPRING.

## SUMMER
This is the season when leafy trees burst with fruit and flowers, and the baby animals of spring grow into adults.

## SPRING
All the action starts in spring! Many plants begin to flower, and many animals breed, so new life can be seen almost everywhere.

SOME ANIMALS CHANGE THEIR COLOUR TO BLEND IN WITH THE SNOW.

## AUTUMN
As the temperature drops, many animals prepare for the winter by storing food and finding a comfy place to shelter.

## WINTER
This is a challenging time of year. The weather can be harsh and food is limited. Some animals go into a deep sleep called hibernation for the whole season.

# WHAT DO I NEED?

Before you head for the great outdoors, be prepared!
First, make sure you think about what to wear and
what to take with you. Go through the checklist
here and keep this book close to hand.

SHORT SLEEVES ARE PERFECT
IN SUMMER, BUT USE SUN
CREAM ON VERY HOT DAYS.

### IN SUMMER
Wear lighter clothing to keep cool in
warm weather and grab your sun hat
if it's a real scorcher. Walking boots
are a must to protect your feet.

## All weathers

Think about where you're going,
and the time of year. Don't forget
to check the weather forecast so
you don't get caught out by a
sudden downpour or a heatwave!

### IN WINTER
Go for a waterproof, windproof jacket over
layers of warm clothing. Wellies are essential
in wet habitats, while hats and gloves will
help you in the snow.

## Collecting samples

If you want a closer look
at use a pooter and a clear
container to collect your
specimen. Remember to
return it to its habitat
afterwards. You can collect
leaves, bark, and flowers
in a plastic pouch.

A POOTER LETS YOU SUCK UP
AN INSECT TO LOOK AT IT
WITHOUT HURTING IT.

PLASTIC POUCH

POOTER

## Binoculars for beginners

Binoculars give you a closer view than you can get with your eyes alone. Spot animals with your eyes first, then use the binoculars to get a better view.

## Checklist

Nature spotting is about watching wildlife, and there are some important items you can take along to help you on your adventures.

☐ **NOTEBOOK, PEN, AND PENCIL**
Sketch any interesting wildlife you see and make notes so you don't forget the details.

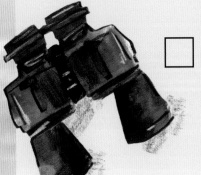

☐ **BINOCULARS**
Binoculars make it easy to watch wildlife from a distance, so you don't disturb the animals.

☐ **MAGNIFYING GLASS**
A handheld magnifying glass is good for getting a better look at plants and insects.

☐ **CAMERA**
Take a camera or mobile phone to take pictures and videos. Use the zoom to get close-up images.

☐ **TORCH**
When nature spotting at night, take a torch to light the way. Some nocturnal insects will also be drawn to the light.

☐ **Don't forget this book.**

### Top tip

AVOID WEARING BRIGHT COLOURS BECAUSE THEY STAND OUT TOO MUCH AND SCARE AWAY WILDLIFE.

PLASTIC CONTAINER

NET

NETS CAN BE USED TO COLLECT FLYING INSECTS AND UNDERWATER ANIMALS.

### Be responsible

Make sure that you act responsibly when you're out enjoying nature. Plan your visits carefully, carry maps, stick to pathways, always read signs, close gates behind you, and never litter.

# HOW DO I SPOT?

To be a true nature detective, you'll need to look up to the sky, down to the ground, and everywhere in between! You'll also need patience – stay still and quiet so animals don't spot you.

### Look for clues

If you can't see any animals, you could search for signs of what has been in the area. Look for pawprints on damp ground, and listen out for birdsongs and other sounds.

## Animal species

This book is full of fascinating species from Britain and northern Europe. Some live all over this area, but others are only found in certain places. Some animals are hard to find because their populations are small, or because they're very good at hiding.

THE EUROPEAN BROWN BEAR LIVES IN A FEW PLACES IN NORWAY, SWEDEN, AND FINLAND.

## Stay safe

WATCH OUT FOR BRIGHT COLOURS IN NATURE. FOR MANY PLANTS AND ANIMALS, THIS CAN BE A WARNING THAT THEY ARE POISONOUS.

## Keep a record

Use a journal to store notes, photographs, and drawings of your nature sightings. Taking notes will let you keep track of how habitats and species change over time.

# WHAT IS IT?

Spotting wildlife can be easy, but identifying exactly what you've seen can be tricky. Each type of plant and animal has unique colours and markings, and some vary depending on their sex and how old they are.

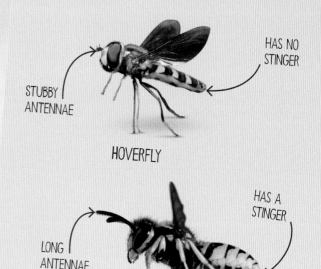

STUBBY ANTENNAE

HAS NO STINGER

HOVERFLY

LONG ANTENNAE

HAS A STINGER

WASP

## Spot the difference

Some animals can look almost identical at first glance. Take notes and photos so you can use an identification guide or website to compare them later on.

DIFFERENT SPECIES IN EACH HABITAT

## A spotter's guide

This book is full of wildlife that you can spot in Britain and northern Europe. There is a picture of each species, and lots of information about it. You'll learn where to find these plants and animals, and get tips on spotting and identification.

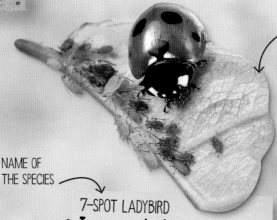

A PICTURE, SO YOU KNOW WHAT TO LOOK OUT FOR

NAME OF THE SPECIES

**7-SPOT LADYBIRD**
**Towns, grasslands**
This ladybird has seven black spots. Its bright colours are a warning to predators that they taste horrible.

LIST OF HABITATS IT IS FOUND IN

FASCINATING PROFILE

## The same but different

Males and females of the same species can look different. Many animals also change their appearance as they get older - just think of tadpoles and frogs!

MALE MANDARIN DUCKS HAVE BRIGHTLY COLOURED FEATHERS TO ATTRACT FEMALES.

ADULT STARLINGS ARE DARK AND SPECKLED, BUT THEIR YOUNG ARE DUSTY BROWN.

### Top tip

REMEMBER THAT SPECIES CAN ALSO LOOK DIFFERENT DEPENDING ON THE TIME OF YEAR. FOR EXAMPLE, SOME STOATS TURN WHITE FOR THE WINTER.

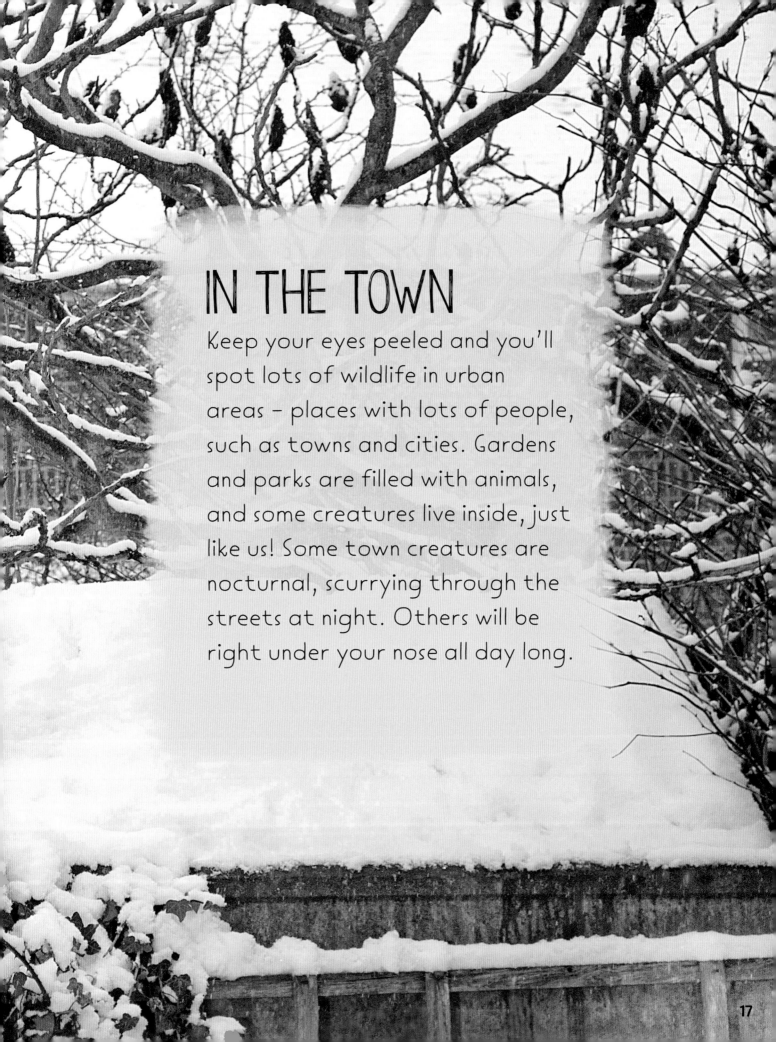

# IN THE TOWN

Keep your eyes peeled and you'll spot lots of wildlife in urban areas – places with lots of people, such as towns and cities. Gardens and parks are filled with animals, and some creatures live inside, just like us! Some town creatures are nocturnal, scurrying through the streets at night. Others will be right under your nose all day long.

## Home away from home

Some animals find homes in town similar to their natural habitats. The city skyline is not that different to the cliffs and treetops where many birds nest in the wild.

### UP ABOVE
Look up and you may spot birds' nests under the edges of roofs, or on high ledges. Birds of prey may also perch up high to look out for food.

THESE WINDOW FRAMES ARE LIKE A CLIFF FACE.

CRACKS IN WALLS AND PAVEMENTS LET WILD FLOWERS TAKE ROOT.

# URBAN LIVING

In towns and cities, wildlife must fight for space with traffic, buildings, and people! Many plants and animals have learned to put up with humans and have found clever ways to survive and thrive alongside us.

IT'S NOT JUST HUMANS WHO LOVE CENTRAL HEATING!

### FAST FOOD
Streets and dumps provide easy pickings for scavengers. This plentiful supply of food makes towns a good home.

### WARM AND SNUG
Many creatures find warmth and shelter in human spaces. Our homes, garages, sheds, attics, or basements make great places to hibernate.

## Food and warmth

The many kitchens and restaurants in a city offer a constant supply of food for animals. Human activity has also made towns warmer than the countryside, perfect for animals who like warmth.

## NOT WELCOME?
Some plants and creatures that share our urban spaces may not be welcome, like weeds in our gardens and spiders in the house. But they are just seeking shelter and food.

## Green corners
Look closely and you'll find lots of mini-habitats around town. Gardens, rivers, parks, balconies, and even walls are all important areas for wildlife to make their homes in.

## Pests or pals?
Don't think of your wildlife neighbours as unwanted visitors. Everything in nature has a purpose – weeds provide nectar for insects, and spiders help keep flies at bay.

NEST BOXES CAN PROVIDE SAFE SPOTS FOR GARDEN BIRDS.

BLUE TIT

## FEARLESS ARRIVAL
Grey squirrels are found across Britain, and often seem fearless of humans. But this animal is not local – it originally came from North America.

FOXGLOVES

HEDGEHOG

## HIDING BELOW
You'll find amphibians around ponds and rivers. In urban areas, garden ponds are an important habitat for frogs and toads.

ROBIN

# ON THE ROOFTOPS

There may be lots of activity on city streets, but the rooftops can be just as busy! Look up and you'll spot birds perching on rooftops and ledges, because they're great places to look for food from.

### CARRION CROW
**Towns, grasslands**
Crows have excellent memories. This helps them remember good places to find food. They can also remember people who are nice to them!

### FERAL PIGEON
**Towns**
You're as likely to find pigeons walking on the street as flying in the sky. It can take less energy to walk than to fly, so it's a good way to get around.

## Rooftop living
Some birds like to nest under the edges of roofs and between the roof tiles. These places are a good substitute for the cracks and crevices in cliffs where these birds would have nested originally.

IT TAKES ABOUT TEN DAYS TO COLLECT ENOUGH MUD TO BUILD A NEST.

### HOUSE MARTIN
**Towns, rivers**
House martins return to our cities every summer. They build nests from little beakfuls of mud gathered nearby, and often reuse the same nest for several years.

SWIFTS ARE SO GOOD AT FLYING THAT THEY CAN DO IT IN THEIR SLEEP!

## SWIFT
**Towns, rivers, coasts**
In summer, you can see swifts swooping and screaming high above other birds. They live life on the wing – feeding, sleeping, and mating while flying.

## HERRING GULL
**Towns, coasts**
Lots of gulls have moved away from the coast and into town. There's plenty of food here that people have thrown away, and fewer predators, too.

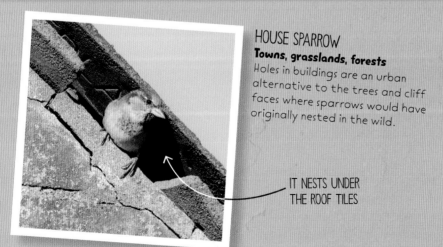

## HOUSE SPARROW
**Towns, grasslands, forests**
Holes in buildings are an urban alternative to the trees and cliff faces where sparrows would have originally nested in the wild.

IT NESTS UNDER THE ROOF TILES

FERAL PIGEONS COME IN LOTS OF SHADES, INCLUDING PALE GREY, BLUE, AND BLACK.

FERAL PIGEON

HERRING GULLS HAVE WHITE UNDERBELLIES AND BLACK WING TIPS.

HERRING GULL

SWIFTS HAVE CRESCENT-SHAPED WINGS AND A FORKED TAIL.

SWIFT

## Be a bird superspotter
There are all sorts of clues to help you identify a bird's species: the shape of its wings and tail, the way it flies, where it's flying, and its markings. Here are some examples of how to identify the birds on this page.

# FEATHERED FRIENDS

Towns have many places for small birds to live, including parks, gardens, hedges, and trees. Gardens with bird feeders and nest boxes are especially popular, because they offer easy food and shelter.

## SCENE SETTER
Hang bird feeders to tempt birds in. Make sure that you place them where they can't be reached by cats.

### BLUE TIT
**Towns, forests**
Blue tits spend 90 per cent of their time foraging for food. They love gardens with bird feeders because it's so easy for them to find food.

### GOLDFINCH
**Towns, forests**
It's easy to spot a goldfinch thanks to its bright red crown and yellow wings. You might see it gobbling seeds from your bird feeder.

### GREAT TIT
**Towns, grasslands, forests**
Great tits change the shape of their beaks during the year, allowing them to eat insects in summer and nuts in winter.

GREAT TITS HAVE BLACK HEADS AND TUMMY STRIPES.

BLUE TIT BOX

ROBIN BOX

SPARROW BOX

## Nest boxes
Birds are very particular about their nests. The size of a nest box, the shape of its opening, and where you place it are all important factors that will determine whether any visitors move in.

### ROBIN
**Towns, forests**
Robins are chirp from before dawn until after dusk. Their songs may sound sweet, but they are warning other robins off their territory!

## STARLING
**Towns, forests**
In winter, starlings meet in flocks. They gather in groups that can number in the millions, all swooping and chattering together.

WATCH FOR THE FLASH OF YELLOW ON ITS WINGS AS IT FLIES.

## GREENFINCH
**Towns, forests**
Many greenfinches now feel at home in urban areas. They are enthusiastic visitors to garden bird feeders or sunflower seed heads.

## BLACKBIRD
**Towns, forests**
You're as likely to see a blackbird on the grass as in a tree. They hop around, cocking their heads to listen for earthworms underground.

## Feed the birds
You can make your garden bird-friendly by growing berry-bearing trees and insect-attracting flowers. In winter, bird feeders are a lifeline for many birds when there is less food available.

USE A MIXTURE OF DIFFERENT SEEDS AND NUTS TO ATTRACT A VARIETY OF BIRDS.

SPARROWHAWKS MAY VISIT YOUR GARDEN TO HUNT SMALLER BIRDS.

THEY RELY ON SURPRISE TO CAPTURE PREY.

BERRY-BEARING PLANTS, SUCH AS CURRANTS, ROWAN, AND HAWTHORN PROVIDE AN IMPORTANT FOOD SUPPLY IN WINTER.

DRIED MEALWORMS MAKE A GOOD MEAL FOR INSECT-EATING BIRDS IN WINTER, WHEN THERE WILL BE FEWER INSECTS IN YOUR GARDEN.

A BAT IS THE ONLY MAMMAL THAT FLIES.

## COMMON PIPISTRELLE
**Towns, forests**
This tiny bat is easier to spot at night, when it comes out to hunt for food. It can catch and eat 3,000 insects in a single night!

# FURRY NEIGHBOURS

Some mammals, such as squirrels, can be bold around humans. Others are more careful, so you'll need to listen out for them. Look for footprints and watch places where they're likely to feed.

HEDGEHOG HIGHWAY

HOLES IN FENCES AND WALLS ALLOW HEDGEHOGS TO TRAVEL MORE FREELY.

## Help a hedgie
The hedgehog population is in decline. Make your garden a hedgie haven by adding a gap in your fence, leaving out a saucer of fresh water, and making a pile of logs and leaves.

## HEDGEHOG
**Towns, forests**
Hedgehogs hibernate – this means they go into a deep sleep through the winter. During the rest of the year, they are active at night.

MAKE OR BUY A HEDGEHOG HOUSE FOR LOCAL HEDGIES TO HIBERNATE IN.

SQUIRRELS HAVE GOOD MEMORIES, BUT THEY CAN STILL FORGET WHERE THEY'VE LEFT THEIR NUT STORES.

## GREY SQUIRREL
**Towns, forests**

You'll spot grey squirrels easily in British towns. They spend their days foraging for food, which they sometimes hide away for the winter.

FOXES COME OUT TO SCAVENGE FOR FOOD AT DAWN AND DUSK.

## BROWN RAT
**Towns, forests**

Brown rats are omnivorous – they eat both plants and meat. Rats can live in most environments, but they are very happy in towns where it's so easy to find food.

## Watch the clock

Some animals, such as squirrels, are diurnal (awake in the day). Others, like mice, are nocturnal (awake at night). Some, like foxes, are crepuscular (active at dawn and dusk).

## RED FOX
**Towns, forests**

Dawn and dusk are the best times to spot urban foxes. This is when they scavenge for food. They'll eat anything, from rats and slugs to rubbish from bins.

BRICKS AND CONCRETE ABSORB THE SUN'S HEAT, HELPING THE PLANT TO GROW.

## SCENE SETTER

Wherever there's a chink in a wall or pavement, a seed can find a way in. Warmth from the Sun on the bricks or concrete will speed up its growth.

## PROCUMBENT YELLOW SORREL
**Towns**
Sorrel seeds explode all over the place in order to scatter and make new plants. This helps sorrel to spread easily.

## DAISY
**Towns, grasslands, forests**
Daisies have been around since the time of the dinosaurs! They have strong roots, and grow everywhere in the world, except Antarctica.

## GREATER PLANTIN
**Towns**
This plant doesn't mind being trampled on – in fact, it usually grows on disturbed ground. It can produce up to 30,000 seeds.

# BETWEEN THE PAVING

People can grow plants in their gardens or window boxes, but some also appear with no help from us. The plants that manage to grow in cities have to be tough to survive.

## SCARLET PIMPERNEL
**Towns**
This plant will look different depending on when you see it. The red flowers open in the morning, and close in the afternoon or in wet weather.

## IVY
**Towns, forests**
This creeping plant provides shelter for birds, bats, and insects. The flowers provide nectar for insects, and holly blue caterpillars eat their buds.

RED ADMIRAL CATERPILLARS EAT NETTLES

## Supporting insects
Gardeners might curse them as "weeds", but urban plants are important for insects. Pavement flowers provide nectar for insects, and their leaves provide food for caterpillars.

RED ADMIRAL BUTTERFLIES LAY EGGS ON NETTLES. THEIR CATERPILLARS EAT THE NETTLES WHEN THEY HATCH.

## DANDELION
**Towns, grasslands, forests**
After its yellow flowers die, they turn into fluffy seedheads. The seeds are blown away by the wind like little parachutes.

LONG ROOTS REACH DEEP FOR WATER AND CAN STORE FOOD.

## COMMON NETTLE
**Towns, grasslands, forests**
Nettles may sting us but animals love them! Caterpillars feast on the leaves, ladybirds scoff the aphids sheltering among them, and birds munch the seeds in autumn.

### COMMON GARDEN SNAIL
**Towns, wetlands, forests**
This snail has two pairs of tentacles just above its mouth. The long pair has eyes at the ends to sense light, and the smaller pair is for smelling.

### GARDEN SPIDER
**Towns, grasslands, forests**
This spider is a super speedy web weaver! It takes only half an hour for it to spin a web around half a metre (2 ft) wide. That's about twice as big as this book!

THIS SPIDER HAS A WHITE CROSS ON ITS BACK.

# BEETLING ABOUT

You'll find all sorts of creepy crawlies around town. These insects, crustaceans, and other small creatures are known as "invertebrates" – animals without a spine.

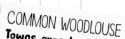

### COMMON WOODLOUSE
**Towns, grasslands, forests**
Woodlice have tough "armour" to hold in moisture. When it's hot outside, they take shelter under rocks to avoid drying out.

### VIOLET GROUND BEETLE
**Towns, grasslands, forests**
These predators hunt slugs, worms, and insects at night. They can often be found resting under logs, stones, and leaves during the day.

THESE BEETLES CAN'T FLY, BUT THEY'RE FAST RUNNERS.

## Insect hotel
Different insects like different habitats to hibernate in. Create a variety of "rooms" in your hotel by filling plant pots with different natural materials, then laying them on their sides.

BAMBOO STICKS

CARDBOARD AND STRAW

DRIED LAVENDER AND SEED HEADS

STICKS AND DRIED LEAVES

## 7-SPOT LADYBIRD
**Towns, grasslands**
This ladybird has seven black spots. Its bright colours are a warning to predators that they taste horrible.

LADYBIRDS HIBERNATE IN WINTER.

## GREY FIELD SLUG
**Towns, wetlands, forests**
A slug's slimy trail is actually mucus, which coats its body to protect it and help it glide along. The slug uses mucus to repel predators too.

THE SLUG CRAWLS ALONG ON ITS MUSCULAR, FLAT, BOTTOM SIDE, CALLED ITS FOOT.

## ZEBRA SPIDER
**Towns, grasslands, forests**
Rather than catching prey in a web, this tiny spider stalks and leaps on its prey. It can jump more than 14 times its body length!

## GREAT POND SNAIL
**Towns, rivers, ponds, wetlands**
This snail grazes on algae just below the surface of water. When it's underwater, it can absorb some oxygen directly into its body through its tentacles.

THIS IS THE LARGEST LAND SNAIL IN EUROPE.

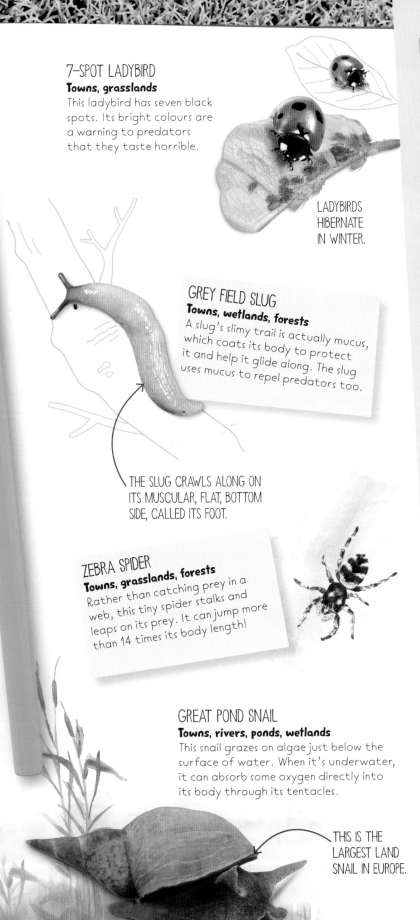

## Microhabitats
Smaller habitats inside larger environments are called "microhabitats". Here are some of the microhabitats you might find in an urban environment.

TREES AND SHRUBS

WALLS

GARDEN PONDS

SOIL

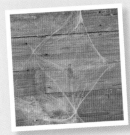
SHEDS

UNDER ROCKS

COMPOST

GREENHOUSES

### PEACOCK BUTTERFLY
**Towns, grasslands, forests**
This butterfly has eyespots on its upperwings to startle predators, who think it's a bigger animal. Peacock butterflies travel far and wide instead of living in one place.

UNLIKE THE BRIGHT UPPERWINGS, THE UNDERWINGS LOOK LIKE DEAD LEAVES.

### SMALL TORTOISESHELL BUTTERFLY
**Towns, grasslands, forests**
In summer, you'll see these butterflies feeding on flowers' nectar. In winter, you might spot them taking shelter in your shed or garuage.

### SCENE SETTER
Plant some flowers in a garden, hanging basket, or window box if you want to attract butterflies to your home. Different butterflies like different plants.

# FLUTTERING BY

On a sunny day butterflies are everywhere, feeding on nectar from their favourite flowers. They lay their eggs on certain plants so that their caterpillar babies have food to eat as soon as they hatch.

## COMMON BLUE BUTTERFLY
**Towns, grasslands**
This small blue butterfly can often be spotted between April and October. Its underwings are actually brown, and the females can be almost completely brown.

## PAINTED LADY BUTTERFLY
**Towns, grasslands, forests**
Painted ladies come to Europe in the summer to lay their eggs. You will spot them from May onwards. In autumn, they migrate to Africa.

## Divided lives
A butterfly's egg hatches into a caterpillar. After eating lots of leaves, it creates a silk cocoon called a chrysalis. Inside the chrysalis, it transforms and then emerges as a butterfly.

EGG

CATERPILLAR

CHRYSALIS

BUTTERFLY

RED ADMIRALS LOVE BASKING IN A SUNNY SPOT.

FLIES HAVE COMPOUND EYES, SO THEY CAN SEE IN ALL DIRECTIONS AT ONCE.

### SILVERFISH

**Towns**

This pest needs starches. That means it eats things in your home such as clothing, paper, carpets, and even wallpaper.

### HOUSEFLIES

**Towns**

The housefly is a food source for many predators, but an unwelcome visitor on our own food, as it can spread diseases.

DIFFERENT SPECIES OF SPIDERS PRODUCE DIFFERENT WEB PATTERNS.

# HIDING INSIDE

We share our homes with many smaller housemates. Originally, they would have lived in caves or other warm spots in the wild, so our homes provide a similar habitat.

## Super spinners

Spider silk is so light that a single strand stretched round the Earth would weigh less than four big bananas. It's also as strong as the material used for bulletproof vests.

THESE BEETLES CAN EAT THROUGH WOODEN BEAMS, FLOORS, AND FURNITURE.

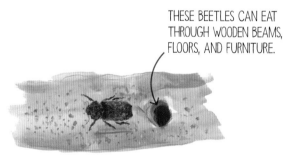

### DEATHWATCH BEETLE

**Towns**

Do you hear something tapping or ticking at night? It could be a male deathwatch beetle bumping its head against the wood in your house to attract a mate.

## ORIENTAL COCKROACH
**Towns**

Most people see cockroaches as pests. They can survive for a month without food, as long as there's water.

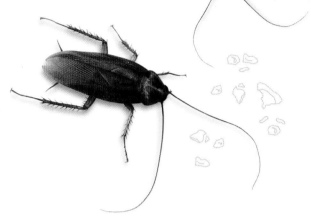

## SCENE SETTER

Buildings – especially the ones with central heating – provide warm, dry, dark habitats for animals, and plenty of stored food.

YOU MIGHT FIND THESE MOTHS IN WARDROBES OR ATTICS.

## DADDY LONGLEGS SPIDER
**Towns**

This spider plucks at other spiders' webs to make them vibrate, tricking the spider into coming out. The daddy longlegs then gobbles them up!

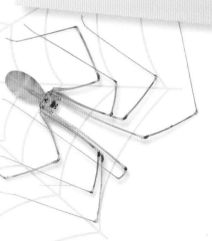

## COMMON CLOTHES MOTH
**Towns**

The moth larvae eat natural fibres, such as wool and cotton. They get all their energy at their larval stage and never eat as adults.

## HOUSE MOUSE
**Towns**

Mice have poor eyesight, but their other senses are very good. Their whiskers detect different surfaces and temperature changes.

YOUNG MICE CAN GET THROUGH A GAP THE WIDTH OF A PENCIL.

# IN THE FIELDS

Vast, open grasslands are found in many parts of Britain and northern Europe. They may look like big empty spaces to you, but for animals they are full of great hiding places. Don't be fooled by the name – grass isn't the only plant that grows here. You'll also find pretty patches of wildflowers and dense hedgerows full of life.

## Open spaces

Farm fields are used for grazing animals, such as cattle. Natural grasslands are left to grow wild, and have more biodiversity (different wildlife).

**GRAZING FIELDS**
Farm animals, such as sheep, cows, and horses all eat grass. They eat a lot of grass, so it is kept very short.

**WILD GRASSLANDS**
Ungrazed grass can grow much taller, providing shelter for all sorts of animals.

# GRASSLAND LIVING

Unlike farmland, nature is left to take its course in grasslands. They still need some attention from humans, though, otherwise they would eventually turn into forests.

**LANDSCAPE OF EUROPE**
Most of Britain and northern Europe was once covered in forest. Over the centuries, people chopped down most of the trees, leaving the grass to grow.

## Grassy planet

Grasslands cover about 30 per cent of the land on Earth. They are found on every continent except for Antarctica.

**WILD FIELDS**
Grasslands usually grow without any help from humans. This natural habitat suits a wide variety of wild flowers, insects, birds, and small mammals.

# Our impact

Human activity has had a huge affect on the grasslands. Our actions have caused problems by changing the climate, reducing the size of this habitat, and harming the wildlife that lives here.

**POLLUTION**
Grasslands can be polluted by chemical pesticides. This tractor is spraying pesticides to protect the crops growing in the farmer's fields.

TREES ARE CHOPPED DOWN TO MAKE SPACE FOR FARMLAND.

**MAKING SPACE**
Large areas of wild grasslands have been cleared to make space for farms. This destroys the native plants and leaves many animals homeless.

**CLIMATE CHANGE**
Climate change can cause unusual weather. Even cooler places like Europe's grasslands can now experience floods, droughts, and fires.

THIS HELICOPTER IS CARRYING WATER TO FIGHT FIRES BLAZING ACROSS THE GRASSLAND.

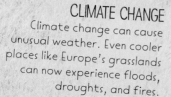

37

# BIRDS OF PREY

You can spot birds of prey swooping, soaring, and hovering in the sky over grasslands. These hunters keep a close watch over the open countryside for moving targets, then fly in to grab their food.

YOU CAN IDENTIFY A HOBBY BY ITS REDDY-BROWN LEGS.

## HOBBY
**Grasslands**
The hobby moves like a graceful acrobat in the air. It needs to be agile to hunt its fast-moving prey, such as dragonflies.

## COMMON BUZZARD
**Grasslands**
Buzzards prey on large animals, such as rabbits and other birds, as well as little earthworms wriggling along on the ground below.

## MERLIN
**Grasslands**
You'll most likely spot merlins flying low over the ground. They prey on other birds, and their hunts can turn into a speedy chase.

ONE OF EUROPE'S SMALLEST BIRDS OF PREY

## SCENE SETTER
The open grasslands give birds of prey a clear view so they can keep an eye out for prey. Nearby woodland provides trees for nesting and resting.

### RED KITE
**Grasslands**

This bird is more of a scavenger than a hunter. It steals food from other birds and eats leftover meat, called carrion.

SPREADS ITS WINGS WIDE TO RIDE WARM CURRENTS IN THE AIR

## On the hunt

Birds of prey all have different ways of hunting. But they all rely on their super senses, powerful bodies, sharp beaks, and strong talons.

POWERFUL BODY AND FORKED TAIL HELP IT TWIST AND TURN

### BEAKS

Birds of prey have powerful beaks. They need to be strong and sharp to tear into fresh meat.

### TALONS

They have sharp, curved claws, called talons. Some of these birds rely more on their talons than their beaks to kill their prey.

### VISION

All these birds have excellent eyesight to help them spot small prey, even from great heights or long distances.

HOVERING GIVES IT LOTS OF TIME TO SCAN THE GROUND

LONG, POINTED WINGS HELP THE KESTREL TO HOVER IN MID-AIR.

### KESTREL
**Grasslands**

Kestrels hover in mid-air, looking for small animals scurrying on the ground. They drop down slowly before pouncing on prey.

**DAY BIRDS**
Tall grass provides a safe place for birds to build their nests. They fly over the grasslands looking for insects, worms, and seeds.

**NORTHERN LAPWING**
**Grasslands**
Lapwings nest in short grass. The males perform dramatic displays of turns and rolls in the sky to attract females.

BLACK AND WHITE COLOURS MAKE IT EASY TO IDENTIFY

# ON THE WING

Grasslands plants provide food for all sorts of different insects. These insects become food for bigger animals themselves, with birds and bats swooping down to eat them up.

LOOK FOR THIS PARTRIDGE'S RED BEAK

MALE SKYLARKS WARBLE SONGS WHILE THEY ARE FLYING.

**SKYLARK**
**Grasslands**
Skylarks nest on the ground. They dig a shallow spot or use a natural hollow, then line it with grass.

**RED-LEGGED PARTRIDGE**
**Grasslands**
Partridges are not very good at flying. You'll probably see them on the ground, where they rummage around for roots and insects.

## STONECHAT
**Grasslands**
This small bird is named after its noisy call, which sounds like two stones banging together. They build grass nests in hedgerows.

MALES HAVE AN ORANGE BREAST

EARS INSIDE ITS HEAD GIVE IT EXCELLENT HEARING

## SHORT-EARED OWL
**Grasslands**
Most people think of owls as birds that live in trees and come out at night. But the short-eared owl hunts in the day and nests on the ground.

## GREATER HORSESHOE BAT
**Grasslands**
This large bat has a horseshoe-shaped flap on its nose. This helps it focus the sound waves that it uses to find its way in the dark.

## SEROTINE BAT
**Grasslands**
This bat catches insects in mid-air. It might stop off in cow fields to eat dung beetles.

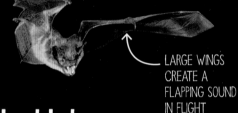

LARGE WINGS CREATE A FLAPPING SOUND IN FLIGHT

# All about bats
Most bats live in woodlands, but some species prefer the grasslands where they can hunt in the open and spot prey easily.

UP ALL NIGHT
Night is a great time to fly around the grasslands unnoticed. There are fewer predators out and about, but lots of small prey to hunt for dinner.

# THE WILDLIFE CORRIDOR

Hedgerows and grassy verges can create a safe, sheltered corridor for woodland animals to cross the grasslands and reach patches of woodland. They also host plants, wildflowers, and juicy fruit.

## HAZEL
**Grasslands, forests**
In spring, you'll spot yellow catkins dangling from hazel branches. By autumn, the catkins have become hazelnuts.

## HAWTHORN
**Grasslands, forests**
This tree has white flowers in summer. Later in the year, it has red berries called haws.

## Trees and shrubs

The tallest plants in hedgerows are trees and shrubs. They provide shelter for many creatures, as well as fruits and nuts for them to eat.

FLOWERS COVER THE TREE, GIVING OFF A SWEET SCENT

## BLACKBERRIES
**Grasslands, forests**
The flowers of this big bramble turn into juicy blackberries – a favourite snack for birds and mice.

## Animals of the hedgerow

Hedgerows have thick vegetation, so they're a safe place for small birds and mammals to hide from predators. There are also lots of fruit, nuts, and insects to eat here.

### HAZEL DORMOUSE
**Grasslands**
This clever little climber builds a neat nest of twigs and grass inside thick hedgerows.

### HARVEST MOUSE
**Grasslands**
The harvest mouse curls its long tail around branches to help it balance.

## How a hedgerow grows

Hedgerows are important habitats that are managed by people. Trees and shrubs are planted on the edges of fields. They grow into hedgerows over time.

**SCENE SETTER**
Thick hedgerows divide up the grasslands into a giant patchwork quilt of fields, meadows, and woodlands.

### HEDGE MUSTARD
**Grasslands**
This tall plant is a great place to spot caterpillars, that come to munch on its leaves.

### GARLIC MUSTARD
**Grasslands, forests**
This flowery plant smells strongly of garlic. It grows in damp, shaded spots, such as hedgerows.

### HEDGE BEDSTRAW
**Grasslands, forests**
The sweet-smelling plant grows best in the shade.

### HEDGE WOUNDWORT
**Grasslands, forests**
You might find the woundwort's purple flowers really stinky, but bees love them!

## Blooming borders

In the soil, under trees and shrubs, are shorter plants. They usually grow in woodlands, but can also survive in hedgerows.

### YELLOWHAMMER
**Grasslands**
It's easy to spot this bird, due to its bright yellow head. You can also identify them from their loud song.

MALES HAVE A GREY HEAD, WHILE FEMALES ARE BROWN.

### WHITETHROAT
**Grasslands**
Male whitethroats are very noisy. They sit on top of the hedgerow and sing a song to attract a mate.

43

# GRASSLAND GRAZERS

Plant-eating animals are happy in grasslands. They can graze on the huge range of plants there whenever they want. Grazing makes the grasses grow back again, so there is rarely a shortage of food.

## SCENE SETTER
The long grass provides a source of food and a place to hide for deer and smaller mammals.

## RED DEER
**Grasslands**
Red deer munch on grass and shrubs. Males, called stags, use their antlers to fight off rivals in mating season.

## FIELD VOLE
**Grasslands**
This noisy little vole makes loud chirping and chattering noises. While grazing, it keeps watch for predators, such as foxes.

## Boxing hares

Spring time is mating season for hares. Females may run away from males or even have a boxing match with them if the males are paying them too much unwanted attention!

FEMALE BROWN HARES STAND TALL ON THEIR HIND LEGS TO BOX TRY-HARD MALES.

### RABBIT
**Grasslands, forests**
Rabbits love gobbling grass and greenery. They live in big groups in homes called burrows that are made up of underground tunnels.

### BROWN HARE
**Grasslands**
Alert and agile, brown hares have keen eyes and good hearing to detect predators. Long legs help them escape at 55 kph (35 mph).

## PYGMY SHREW
**Grasslands**
This tiny mammal weighs less than a small coin! Despite its small size, it makes a lot of noise, squeaking as it fights other shrews.

ITS LARGE, POINTY NOSE GIVES IT A STRONG SENSE OF SMELL.

## STOAT
**Grasslands, forests**
Stoats are normally brown. Some turn white in winter, but only in northern countries, such as Scotland.

STOATS STAND UP TO CHECK THE AREA FOR PREDATORS.

# GRASSLAND HUNTERS

Grasslands provide an open hunting ground. These predators are carnivores – they eat other animals. They can also be hunted and become prey for other animals.

COLD-BLOODED LIZARDS MUST LIE IN THE SUNSHINE TO WARM UP.

## SLOW WORM
**Grasslands**
Slow worms look like snakes but they are actually legless lizards. Females have about eight wriggly babies in the summer.

## COMMON LIZARD
**Grasslands**
This is the UK's most common reptile. It can escape predators by shedding its tail and growing a new one.

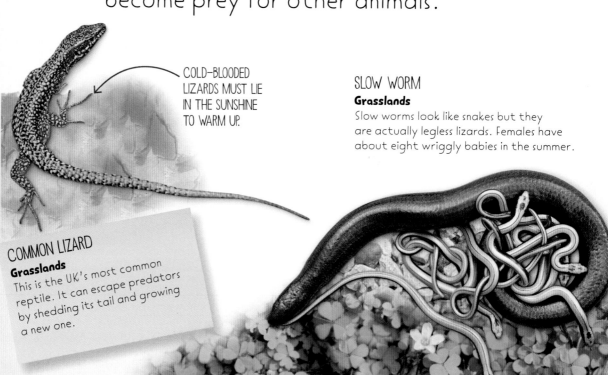

## ADDER
**Grasslands**
This is the only venomous snake in northern Europe. It injects venom into its prey through its fangs.

MOLES HAVE SHORT, VELVET-LIKE FUR.

## EUROPEAN MOLE
**Grasslands**
Molehills scattered over the countryside show where moles have been digging underground tunnels and feasting on juicy worms.

A ZIGZAG PATTERN CAMOUFLAGES THE ADDER, MAKING IT HARD TO SPOT.

SHED SNAKESKIN IN THE GRASS

IN SOME REGIONS, ITS SOFT BROWN AND WHITE FUR TURNS WHITE IN WINTER.

## LEAST WEASEL
**Grasslands, forests**
These animals are smaller than stoats, and full of energy. They race around grasslands on the lookout for voles, their main source of food.

## Shedded snakeskin
You may find a snakeskin on a grassland walk. Adders and grass snakes shed their skin as they grow. They grow a new layer of skin underneath, so they are always protected.

LONG ANTENNAE HELP THE
MOTH FEEL ITS WAY AROUND.

### SIX-SPOTTED BURNET
**Grasslands**
This moth has bright red spots to
tell predators it is dangerous. If
under attack, it releases chemicals
that make it taste bad.

### MEADOW BROWN
**Grasslands**
Unlike most other butterflies,
meadow browns don't mind
flying on cloudy days. They are
active from late summer to
early autumn.

# BUZZING AND BEATING

Buzzing bees and fluttering wings are the sounds
of summer in the grasslands. It's a great time of
year for spotting insects as they visit wild flowers
to feed on their nectar.

### BEES
**Grasslands**
Busy bees buzz around to collect
nectar. They use some of the nectar
to make honey, which they eat
during the colder months.

### SMALL COPPER
**Grasslands**
The male butterflies each have
their own territory, and will chase
off other insects that come into
their space.

## SCENE SETTER

From a distance, the grasslands look calm and quiet. But get a little closer and you'll hear thousands of insects flying from flower to flower.

## HOVERFLIES

**Grasslands**

Although hoverflies are harmless, they look like wasps. This disguise makes predators think they are dangerous and so they avoid them.

## DARK GREEN FRITILLARY

**Grasslands**

This butterfly can fly very fast, flitting between flowers to feed on nectar.

## WASPS

**Grasslands**

Wasps look similar to bees, but are thinner and less furry. They are often more angry and aggressive, and can sting more than once.

# Why are butterflies so colourful?

Butterflies have many predators, including birds, wasps, and spiders. Their bright colours can help them camouflage, warn predators that they could be dangerous to eat, and also help to attract a mate.

A PEACOCK BUTTERFLY CAMOUFLAGES ITSELF BY CLOSING ITS WINGS, HIDING THE BRIGHT EYE SPOTS.

## RINGLET

**Grasslands, forests**

These butterflies start out almost black after emerging from their chrysalis. They become lighter brown as they get older.

### HORSESHOE VETCH
**Grasslands**
This plant is known as a "perennial". That means it can live for many years, surviving even the coldest winters or dry summer seasons.

### SCENE SETTER
Wild flowers grow all over the grasslands. Wherever there are flowers, there are insects, because flowers and insects need each other to survive.

# THE POLLEN STATION

Have you ever seen insects flitting from flower to flower? They are busy looking for sweet nectar to eat. At the same time, they help the plants to spread their pollen far and wide.

## What is pollen?
Pollen grows in flowers, and is needed to make seeds. Pollen has to be spread around to make seeds, but because plants can't move they often need the help of insects to get the job done.

BE CAREFUL OF ITS SPIKY LEAVES.

### COMMON KNAPWEED
**Grasslands**
Gardeners and farmers consider this plant to be a weed. But it produces a lot of nectar for insects to eat.

### RED ADMIRAL
**Grasslands, towns, forests**
You can spot red admirals almost everywhere! Look out for them on warm, sunny days, when they fly around feasting on flowers.

**TINY YELLOW FLORETS**

## OXEYE DAISY
**Grasslands**
Each white petal is attached to a tiny yellow flower called a "floret". So the top of the daisy isn't just one flower, but many!

THIS BEE IS GETTING DUSTED WITH POLLEN AS IT FEEDS ON THE FLOWER'S NECTAR.

## Fragrant flowers
Flowers smell good so they can attract pollinators (animals that help to spread pollen). An insect comes to eat the nectar, and pollen gets dusted onto its legs. When it visits a new plant, the pollen is left behind.

**BEES CAN STING! WATCH THEM FROM A SAFE DISTANCE.**

**TINY HAIRS**

**FLOWER BUD**

## FIELD POPPY
**Grasslands**
Poppies are known as "annual" plants. Their life cycle lasts one year, so they need to grow, flower, and spread their seeds quickly.

## CORNFLOWER
**Grasslands**
This pretty plant used to be common in fields, but is now endangered in the wild. This is because farms now cover most of its natural habitat.

**RAGGED LEAF SHAPE**

## MARBLED WHITE
**Grasslands**
These butterflies can be spotted in large groups in the summer, when the weather is sunny and warm.

# MUCKING AROUND

At ground level in the grasslands, insects make the most of the rich soil, lush plants, and plentiful prey. Beetles scuttle and scurry, while crickets and grasshoppers produce chirping sounds in the summer.

## SOLDIER BEETLE
**Grasslands**
This beetle gets its name from its red and black colours, which look a bit like a soldier's uniform. It uses its strong jaws to eat insects.

## CLICK BEETLE
**Grasslands, towns**
Click beetles are known for their jumps, but they don't actually leap with their legs. An internal joint helps them spring into action.

## DARK BUSH CRICKET
**Grasslands**
This skilled jumper uses its long legs to leap across the grasslands in search of plants and insects to eat.

## ROSE CHAFER BEETLE
**Grasslands, towns**
Shimmering in the summer sunlight, the rose chafer beetle crawls through the wild flowers, feeding on leaves, petals, and nectar.

## DUNG BEETLE
**Grasslands**
This beetle eats poo to survive. It lives inside dung piles near cattle, or it tunnels into the soil looking for poo left by other creatures.

### FIELD CRICKET
**Grasslands**
Crickets chirp by rubbing their wings together. They live underground in burrows. They jump huge distances to escape danger.

### OIL BEETLE
**Grasslands**
Never mess with an oil beetle! If disturbed, it produces a poisonous liquid that causes blisters – so it's also called a "Blister Beetle".

### COMMON GREEN GRASSHOPPER
**Grasslands**
This bright green grasshopper blends in with its grassy home. It makes a loud chirping noise by rubbing its legs and wings together.

### MEADOW GRASSHOPPER
**Grasslands**
You might hear this grasshopper before you see it. Males have long wings, but the wings of female meadow grasshoppers are short.

DEER

CARRION CROW

FRONT PAW

BACK PAW

SQUIRREL

## Animal tracks
Looking for animal tracks in mud or soil is a good way to find out which creatures have passed through. Tracks look different depending on the visitor, but the more you see, the more you'll learn to recognize.

# HEATHS AND MOORS

These wide open spaces have strong winds and soil that is low in nutrients, so only the toughest plants survive. Snakes slither around this remote habitat, and many birds nest on the ground.

## GORSE
**Heathlands**

The dazzling yellow flowers of this thorny plant brighten up the heathland habitat. Gorse grows very quickly, even in bad soil.

## SMOOTH SNAKE
**Heathlands**

This shiny smooth snake hunts down lizards, rodents, and insects in the heathlands. It bites hard but isn't venomous.

DARK COLOURS AND MARKINGS HELP THE SNAKE HIDE.

## HEATHER
**Heathlands**

Every year, this tough, evergreen plant grows sweet-smelling flowers, beautifully transforming the heathlands.

SUMMER FLOWERS CAN BE PURPLE, PINK, OR WHITE.

## BLACK GROUSE
**Heathlands, moorlands**

Heather provides grouse with food to eat and a place to nest. In mating season, males show off their black feathers to females.

# Spot the difference

Heathlands are dry and windy places where only strong plants grow. Moorlands are usually on higher ground with wet weather and damp soil. This means that the same plants cannot grow in both habitats.

HEATHER CREATES A CARPET OF COLOUR ALL OVER THE HEATHLANDS.

MUDDY BOGS AND SOGGY SOIL ARE TYPICAL IN MOORLANDS.

## EUROPEAN NIGHTJAR
**Heathlands, moorlands**
At dusk, the nightjar comes out to hunt, catching flying insects in its open mouth. It nests in hollows on the ground.

STICKY DEW TRAPS INSECTS.

## ROUND-LEAVED SUNDEW
**Moorlands**
The sundew is not just a pretty plant – it is also a deadly trap! It feeds on insects that get stuck on the hairs of its leaves.

PURPLE MOOR-GRASS GROWS IN WET BOGS.

## EXMOOR PONY
**Moorlands**
Ponies have lived on British moors for centuries. The Exmoor pony is the toughest, with a thick coat, powerful body, and strong legs.

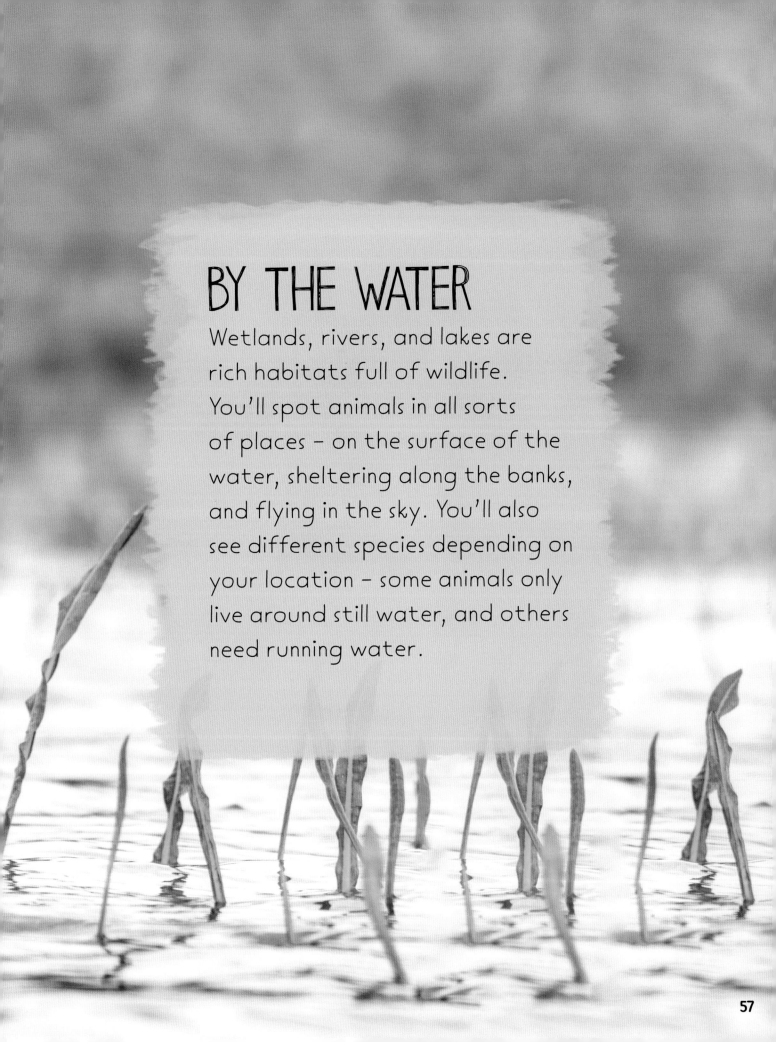

# BY THE WATER

Wetlands, rivers, and lakes are rich habitats full of wildlife. You'll spot animals in all sorts of places – on the surface of the water, sheltering along the banks, and flying in the sky. You'll also see different species depending on your location – some animals only live around still water, and others need running water.

# FRESHWATER LIVING

Freshwater habitats are different to the salty seawater habitats along the coast. Some are natural, others are artificial (made by people).

## Water bodies

Freshwater habitats come in many forms. They include calm lakes, mucky bogs, and rivers heading out to sea.

### ARTIFICIAL WATERWAYS

It's not always just nature that makes freshwater habitats. Rivers can be dammed to make lakes and reservoirs, and canals cut into the land provide artificial waterways.

### NATURE'S COURSE

As a river flows, it cuts a channel through the earth, eroding the soil and carving a path to the sea.

### WONDERFUL WETLANDS

Wetlands are areas of land that get flooded, either temporarily or permanently.

## Supporting life

Still water habitats, such as lakes, have a different ecosystem (wildlife network) compared to habitats with running water, such as rivers.

### STILL OR RUNNING WATER
Some species only live in one type of habitat, either still or running water. Others, such as otters, can be found in both.

### BUG BUFFET
As still water is a breeding ground for many insects, crustaceans, and worms, it offers a feast for wading birds, such as snipe.

## Pollution problem

Ponds, lakes, and slow rivers can easily become choked with rubbish or poisoned with chemicals that cannot flow away. These pollutants harm the wildlife as they build up.

### ALGAL BLOOM
Fertilizers from farm fields make algae grow quickly into thick clumps. They smother the natural plants, which die and rot, fouling the water.

### THAT'S RUBBISH
Litter can break down to release tiny plastic particles and chemicals that harm food chains.

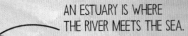
AN ESTUARY IS WHERE THE RIVER MEETS THE SEA.

59

## KINGFISHER

**Rivers**

Keep your eyes peeled and you might spot this bird perched on a low-hanging branch. From here, it dives into the water to catch small fish.

## DAUBENTON'S BAT

**Rivers**

Watch out for these bats at dusk or dawn. They flick insects in the air with their tails and scoop them up in their mouths.

SPOT THEM SKIMMING
OVER THE WATERLINE.

# OVER THE WATER

Just above the surface of the water is where many insects breed and feed. Watch carefully and you might spot predators swooping and diving over the water hunting for an insect dinner.

## MAYFLY

**Rivers, lakes**

As adults, these insects don't have working mouthparts. This means they cannot feed and do not live long. They mate before their short adult lives are over.

MOST MAYFLIES
ONLY LIVE FOR
A FEW DAYS.

## SCENE SETTER

Midday is a good time to go nature spotting on the water, because animals like kingfishers and dragonflies will be out looking for food.

## DAMSELFLY
**Rivers**
You can identify damselflies because they rest with their wings closed, while similar-looking dragonflies rest with their wings open.

MALES ARE BLUE, WHILE FEMALES ARE GREEN.

## EMPEROR DRAGONFLY
**Rivers, lakes**
This dragonfly's spectacular flying skills mean it can hover in mid-air, speed up quickly, and fly in any direction to attack its prey.

## WHITE-THROATED DIPPER
**Rivers**
You can spot dippers bobbing up and down on stones in fast-flowing water. They can walk underwater to catch their prey.

DIPPERS EAT UNDERWATER INVERTEBRATES.

## Dinner time
When you see these birds, bats, and insects over water, it means they're probably hunting for food. Here are some of the things these animals like to eat.

### NON-BITING MIDGE
**Rivers, lakes**
These midges look like mosquitoes, but they don't bite. They are prey for Daubenton's bats and some dragonflies.

### MINNOW
**Rivers**
Minnows group together in a shoal for protection, and are constantly alert to danger from every angle.

### MOSQUITO
**Lakes, towns**
They may be annoying blood-suckers to humans, but mosquitoes themselves are food for lots of other animals.

# ON THE RIVER BANK

Wait patiently by a river bank and you'll see lots of wildlife. What you see depends on how fast the water's flowing. Some species prefer fast-flowing rivers, others like calmer, slow-moving water, and some are happy in both.

### WATER VOLE
**Rivers, lakes**
Voles will munch a "lawn" of grass in front of their riverbank burrows, so look for piles of nibbled grass and stems by the water's edge.

### OTTER
**Rivers, wetlands**
It's not easy to spot otters – excellent senses alert them to danger, so they will run if they hear or smell you coming.

### MEADOWSWEET
**Rivers, wetlands**
To spot this plant, look out for its frothy, cream-coloured flowers on tall stems. You can also try to sniff it out by its sweet smell.

A THICK, DENSE COAT OF FUR KEEPS OTTERS WARM IN COLD WATER.

## GREY HERON
**Rivers, lakes, wetlands**
You're most likely to spot a heron standing like a statue in shallow water, watching patiently for its next fish or frog meal to swim by.

HERONS HAVE A WINGSPAN NEARLY AS WIDE AS A CAR.

BEAVERS GNAW THROUGH TREES TO GET BRANCHES TO BUILD THEIR DAMS WITH.

## Nature's engineers
Beavers are wetland heroes, building dams to create ponds. This creates habitats for lots of other animals. Dams also reduce flooding and improve water quality.

## WATER MINT
**Rivers, wetlands**
Water mint smells like toothpaste when its leaves are crushed. Small butterflies love its clusters of lilac-pink flowers.

## BEAVER
**Rivers**
Beavers are adapted to both land and water with webbed feet, a see-through third eyelid to use underwater, and a big flat tail. This tail helps beavers live both on land and in water.

# IN AND OUT OF WATER

Ponds may be quiet in winter, as many of these animals sleep through it. In spring, ponds burst to life again as the animals come out to breed, and in summer there are all kinds of animal activity!

## GRASS SNAKE
**Rivers, lakes, wetlands**
You might spot one of these talented swimmers gliding through open water from spring to autumn. In winter, they hibernate.

## COMMON TOAD
**Lakes, wetlands**
After winter hibernation, toads set out on a dangerous migration to the ponds where they breed, often crossing busy roads to get there.

## COMMON FROG
**Lakes, wetlands**
On summer evenings, you can spot frogs coming out to hunt. But in winter, they hibernate under logs or in the muddy bottoms of ponds.

## What's the difference?

Common toads and common frogs look a lot alike! So how do you tell them apart? Here are a few key ways to tell the difference:

- Location: Toads like dry ground, as their skin is more waterproof, but frogs lose moisture more easily, so stay near water.

- Action: Frogs hop around, while toads prefer to crawl.

- Size: Frogs are usually smaller than toads.

- Legs: Frogs have long legs – longer than their head and body. Toads, on the other hand, have much shorter legs.

- Face: Frogs have a more pointed nose, while a toad's is wider.

- Skin: Frogs have smoother skin, while toads are covered in bumps.

## Water babies

Frogs, toads, and newts give birth to eggs, called spawn, which hatch into swimming larvae, called tadpoles. The larvae then grow into adults that can walk on land and swim in water.

THESE TADPOLES WILL SPROUT LEGS AND ARMS AS THEY SLOWLY GROW INTO ADULTS.

### SMOOTH NEWT
**Wetlands, grasslands**
By day, smooth newts hide under logs or stones. By night, they hunt insects and slugs on land, or insects, shrimps, and tadpoles in water.

### GREAT CRESTED NEWT
**Wetlands**
This newt is very rare. The males develop a wavy crest which they use to attract females, along with some fancy dance-like moves.

### FIRE SALAMANDER
**Wetlands, forests**
These striking yellow markings act as a warning to predators. This salamander spends more time on land than these other amphibians.

### PALMATE NEWT
**Wetlands, heathlands**
Like all newts, this tiny newt is born in the water, but it soon moves to live on land. It then returns to water to lay its eggs.

# BOBBING ABOUT

With waterproof feathers to keep them warm and dry, these birds can spend their days happily in and around the water, dabbling and diving for food.

## SCENE SETTER
Water birds are well-adapted to life on the water. They can even take off and land on water.

## MALLARD
**Rivers, lakes, wetlands**
Like many waterfowl, mallards stick their head underwater with their tail in the air to help them find food. This is called "upending".

## MUTE SWAN
**Rivers, lakes**
Mute swans mostly eat plants that grow in shallow waters, so they upend rather than diving completely underwater.

## GREAT CRESTED GREBE
**Rivers, lakes, coasts**
Grebes seem clumsy on land, but they're great at diving. They'll often dive to escape predators, rather than flying away.

YOUNG GREBES RIDE ON THEIR PARENTS' BACKS.

# Made for the water

Waterfowl are well adapted to life on and around the water. Their bills, feet, and feathers all help them thrive in this watery habitat.

MANY DUCKS FEED BY DABBLING: UPENDING IN THE WATER TO FEED WITH THEIR HEADS UNDER THE SURFACE.

WEBBED FEET ALLOW THESE BIRDS TO SWIM THROUGH THE WATER AND KEEP THEIR BALANCE ON LAND.

A DUCK'S "PREEN" GLAND PRODUCES OIL TO COAT ITS FEATHERS, MAKING THEM WATERPROOF.

## TUFTED DUCK
**Lakes, wetlands**
Tufted ducks dive so suddenly that they almost seem to disappear. Males are almost black, and females are brown.

TUFT IS SHORTER IN WINTER THAN IN SUMMER.

## COOT
**Rivers, lakes**
Coots are omnivorous. They dive for food, but bring their catch to the surface before eating it.

**RAFT SPIDER**
**Lakes, ponds, wetlands, heathlands**
Raft spiders can run across the water to chase their prey, or dive down and swim underwater to escape danger.

IT CAN ALSO BE FOUND ON FLOATING PLANTS, OR AT THE WATER'S EDGE.

**PIRATE WOLF SPIDER**
**Rivers, lakes, ponds, wetlands**
This spider senses its prey's movements on the water's surface, then either chases it down or waits to ambush it.

FEMALES CARRY A SILK-LINED COCOON FOR THEIR EGGS.

# AT THE SURFACE

Look closely at the waterline and you'll see it's full of animal activity. This is also a prime hunting ground for animals that can hunt on or under the water.

## Under the water

Fearsome, tiny predators lurk just under the waterline as well as on the surface. You'll only see them if you manage to scoop them up in a net. But be careful, some species can bite!

COMMON BACKSWIMMER
**Rivers, ponds, wetlands**
This insect uses its oar-like legs to swim upside-down just below the surface, and surprises unsuspecting prey.

**POND SKATER**
**Rivers, lakes, ponds, wetlands**
These insects can be seen skating over the surface of the water, hunting for small insects by detecting vibrations on the water.

## How do they do it?
These animals can walk on water thanks to the hairs on their undersides or legs. These hairs repel (push back) water and support their weight as they run, walk, skate, or sit on the water's surface.

IT MOVES MORE SLOWLY ON THE WATER THAN A POND SKATER.

**WHIRLIGIG BEETLE**
**Rivers, lakes, ponds**
With back legs like paddles and eyes that can see above and below water at the same time, the whirligig is a well-adapted surface hunter.

IT MAINLY PREYS ON ANIMALS THAT FALL IN THE WATER.

**WATER MEASURER**
**Rivers, lakes, ponds, wetlands**
These spindly animals may look fragile, but they're actually fierce predators. They spear prey with their needle-like mouthparts.

**WATER SCORPION**
**Rivers, ponds, wetlands**
This underwater predator lurks among dead leaves, using its scorpion-like tail as a snorkel to breathe underwater as it waits to ambush its prey.

### THREE-SPINED STICKLEBACK
**Rivers, lakes, ponds, wetlands**
Three sharp spines on its back give
this fierce predator its name. It latches
onto its prey with tiny, sharp teeth.

MALES HAVE RED UNDERSIDES
DURING BREEDING SEASON.

### NON-BITING MIDGE LARVAE
**Lakes, ponds, wetlands**
These larvae will eventually
turn into pupae that swim
to the surface and transform
into flying insects.

# UNDERWATER
Beneath the water's surface there's a whole
new world of animals. Here are some of the
species you're most likely to find when you
go pond dipping.

### Stay safe
WHEN YOU GO POND DIPPING,
TAKE IT SLOW SO YOU DON'T
SLIP ON WET ROCKS. DON'T
WADE TOO FAR OUT INTO A
POND, LAKE, OR RIVER.

### TADPOLE
**Lakes, ponds**
These tadpoles will eventually
become frogs. Their gills are
replaced with lungs as
they get bigger.

### WATER HOG-LOUSE
**Lakes, ponds**
The water hog-louse is most
common at the bottom of ponds,
where there are lots of decaying
leaves. They feed on rotting plants
and animals.

# Pond dipping

You'll need a net, a magnifying glass, and a small tub filled with pond water. Gently drag the net through the water, then empty it into the tub to identify your catch. Put the animals back when you've finished looking at them.

REMEMBER TO WEAR RUBBER BOOTS SO YOU CAN GET INTO THE WATER.

## GREAT DIVING BEETLE
**Lakes, ponds**
This predator sticks the tip of its body out of the water to renew its air supply, which it stores under its wings.

HIDES UNDER STONES AND LEAVES

## FRESHWATER SHRIMP
**Rivers, lakes, ponds**
Because their bodies naturally curve into a C-shape, freshwater shrimp tend to swim on their sides when they are not hiding from predators.

POND SNAILS HAVE SWIRLY SHELLS THAT END IN A POINT.

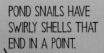

RAMSHORN SHELLS ARE A FLAT COIL.

## FLATWORM
**Rivers, lakes, ponds, wetlands**
Gliding along a bit like slugs, flatworms hunt for small snails and worms. You can tempt them out with a bit of raw meat on a string.

## RAMSHORN SNAIL
**Rivers, lakes, ponds, wetlands**
Like pond snails, ramshorn snails have a lung for breathing, so they occasionally come up to the surface for air.

**MARSH FRITILLARY**
**Wetlands, moorlands**
You might spot this rare butterfly feeding on marsh marigold nectar. Its caterpillars are black and fuzzy-looking.

**MARSH MARIGOLD**
**Wetlands, lakes**
An important spring flower for wildlife, this water-dwelling plant offers shelter to frogs and early nectar to insects.

# WETLANDS

Wetlands are areas of land that get flooded, either temporarily or permanently. Marshes, peat bogs, reedbeds, and fens all offer different habitats for wildlife.

IT ALSO NESTS ON ROOFTOPS IN TOWNS.

**EUROPEAN WHITE STORK**
**Wetlands, towns**
This tall, white stork has a long red beak and legs. It stalks along, foraging for small mammals, fish, amphibians, and large insects.

**COMMON SNIPE**
**Wetlands, grasslands, moorlands**
In spring, male snipes put on flight displays to attract mates. The air rushing through their tail feathers makes a "drumming" sound.

LONG BEAK TO EAT INSECTS IN THE MUD

**WILD ANGELICA**
**Wetlands, rivers, forests**
This giant marshland plant can grow taller than you! Its clusters of purple-tinged flowers provide food for many insects.

THIS PLANT IS RELATED TO THE CARROT.

## COMMON REED
**Wetlands, rivers, lakes, coasts**
Reedbeds are big patches of wet habitat that contain common reeds and not much else! These tall plants offer cover for birds.

## BITTERN
**Wetlands**
This master of camouflage hunts among the reeds. On spring evenings, the male hoots a foghorn-like "boom" to attract a mate.

## REED BUNTING
**Wetlands, grasslands**
These birds build nests near the ground. Males have brown heads in the winter but change colour for the breeding season.

MALES HAVE BLACK HEADS IN THE BREEDING SEASON.

## EUROPEAN REED WARBLER
**Wetlands**
After spending winter in Africa, the reed warbler comes north to breed, building its basket-like nest between reed stalks.

# Mossy bog
Sphagnum mosses are warriors in the fight against climate change. They grow over thick layers of peat (decaying plants), which stops the peat from rotting further and releasing its trapped carbon into the air.

SOME MOSSES WERE ALSO USED AS WOUND DRESSINGS DURING WORLD WAR I.

# ON THE COAST

There's more to the coast than just the seashore. There are also salt marshes, mudflats, and estuaries where rivers meet the sea. Spotting animals here is an exciting adventure. You might have to tackle tricky terrain and wild weather, but you'll be rewarded with some incredible wildlife sightings.

# COASTAL LIVING

What do you picture when you think of the coast? It's not just beaches. There are inland habitats such as marshes and estuaries, too. Coasts are home to a wide range of plants and animals.

**MUDDY SHORE**
These are nutrient-rich habitats and are sometimes covered in salt marsh plants. Many birds wander these shores, hunting for food in the damp ground.

## Different shores
The shore is the land next to the sea. There are several types of shores depending on what they're made up of. Each animal has its favourite type of shore.

**ROCKY SHORE**
Here, the shoreline is made up of solid rock. Craggy rocks can collect seawater, forming rock pools. These are unique microhabitats, filled with sea life.

GULLS GATHER IN NOISY FLOCKS.

**SANDY SHORE**
On sandy beaches, all sorts of animals live underground, burrowing down into the sand. Birds hunt for them, probing into the sand with their beaks.

**SHINGLE SHORE**
Shingle beaches are also rocky, but they are made up of small stones compared to the big boulders and cliffs of rocky shores.

# Changing scenery

Coastal habitats change over the course of the day due to the tides. You'll also find different animals at certain times of year, because some animals only visit in particular seasons.

## TIDAL TIME
At high tide (when the tide comes in), more of the shore is covered with water. At low tide, more land is revealed, along with rock pools.

## THROUGH THE YEAR
Some birds spend whole seasons in different places. You will see different species on the coast in the winter to those you will spot in the summer.

## DEFENDING THE COAST
Have you spotted wooden, artificial barriers along the shore? They are called "groynes". They stop the tides from carrying sediment away, which slows beach erosion.

SEA PLANTS, SUCH AS GREEN ALGAE, GET WASHED UP ON THE BEACH BY THE TIDES.

# Climate change

Climate change causes sea levels to rise, so coasts get eroded or flooded. Plants and animals that live along the coast struggle to adapt to these changes in their habitat.

# CLIFFHANGERS

Crumbly cliffs can be dangerous places for humans, but for some animals they're places of safety. Seabirds make nests on cliffs because it's harder for predators to reach them there.

**ARCTIC TERN**
**Coasts**
Arctic terns share the skies with other coastal birds, but they nest on the ground rather than on cliffs.

SEA THRIFT FLOWERS

WINGS FOR BOTH SWIMMING AND FLYING

**RAZORBILL**
**Coasts**
Razorbills are usually found at sea, bobbing in the water or diving for fish. They usually only come on land to breed and look after their chicks.

## Cliff plants

Plants that grow on coastal cliffs need to be strong enough to handle bright sunshine, fierce winds, and salty sea spray. To survive all this, they often have sturdy stems, tough leaves, and small flowers.

**SEA THRIFT**
**Coasts, salt marshes**
This flower comes from coastal areas, but it's also a popular garden plant. It's evergreen, which means it stays green all year long.

**ROCK SAMPHIRE**
**Coasts**
This plant is actually a type of wild carrot that some people like to eat. It grows high up on dry rocks, so the plant's fat leaves store lots of water.

## Stay safe

BE CAREFUL WHEN YOU GO ON A CLIFFTOP WALK. ALWAYS STAY AWAY FROM THE EDGE AND LOOK OUT FOR SIGNS THAT WARN OF DANGEROUS SPOTS.

CLIFF EDGES CAN CRUMBLE INTO THE SEA.

### ATLANTIC PUFFIN
**Coasts**
Puffins are easy to spot because of their stripy orange beak and black-and-white markings. They nest in burrows, which they dig on cliffs.

### KITTIWAKE
**Coasts**
Kittiwake nests are made from seaweed stuck together with mud and droppings. They nest together in large colonies, so their homes can be very noisy.

### GANNET
**Coasts**
Gannets are specially adapted to dive for food. They have air pockets around their necks, stomachs, and sides that act as cushions when they hit the water.

### COMMON GUILLEMOT
**Coasts**
These birds don't build nests. Instead, the female guillemot lays a single, pointy egg on a rocky ledge. She then stands guard over it.

### KIDNEY VETCH
**Coasts**
The flowers of the kidney vetch can be yellow or red. It's easiest to spot this plant when its flowers bloom in summer. It grows high up on rocky cliffs.

### CORMORANT
**Coasts, rivers**
Cormorants build nests from seaweed. You can often spot them standing with their wings open, drying off after a dive.

# ROCKY SHORES

Rock pools are found in the intertidal zone. This area of land is high and dry at low tide and underwater at high tide. At low tide, small pools of water can be left behind on the shore.

### SHORE CRAB
**Coasts**
These crabs can grow to be 10 cm (4 in) wide. They have five spikes on each side of their carapace (shell).

### GREEN SEA URCHIN
**Coasts**
Sea urchins may look like spiky plants, but they are animals. They need to be underwater to survive, so they live in lower shore areas.

## Shore zones

Rocky shores are split into zones. Each zone spends a different amount of time in water and in air, depending on the tides. This is an example of high tide.

THE SUBTIDAL ZONE IS ALWAYS COVERED IN WATER, EVEN AT LOW TIDE.

THE LOWER SHORE IS UNDERWATER LONGER THAN THE UPPER SHORE.

**Subtidal zone**

**Lower shore**

## YELLOW LICHEN
**Coasts, forests**
This plant needs to stay out of water to survive, so it lives higher up the shore in areas that are not usually covered at high tide.

## BLADDER WRACK SEAWEED
**Coasts**
Round air bubbles in this seaweed's fronds help it float to the surface so it can reach the sunlight it needs to stay alive.

## COMMON STARFISH
**Coasts**
Starfish are one of the top shoreline predators. They eat mussels and clams by dissolving them in their stomach's digestive juices.

## BEADLET ANEMONE
**Coasts**
These bright red creatures have strong suckers that keep them anchored to rocks while they are battered by the waves.

## Rock pool viewers
Make a rock pool viewer to see wildlife without disturbing it. Take a plastic tube 10 cm (4 in) wide, and trace a circle around it on a clear piece of plastic. Cut out the circle and glue it to one end of the tube. (You may need an adult to help you, as the plastic may be hard to cut.) Then dip your viewer into the water and take a look!

WAVES HIT THE MIDDLE SHORE HARDEST.

THE UPPER SHORE IS THE HIGHEST LIMIT OF THE TIDE.

THE SPLASH ZONE IS NEVER UNDERWATER, EVEN AT HIGH TIDE.

**Middle shore**

**Upper shore**

**Splash zone**

# ON THE DUNES

Sand dunes can be found on the beach or a little further back from the shoreline. Only a few plants are able to survive in the salty ground, and unique wildlife lives there.

### SAND LIZARD
**Coasts, heathlands**
In spring, male sand lizards turn bright green to attract mates. Females are brown for camouflage against the sand.

### CINNABAR MOTH
**Coasts**
This pretty insect looks like a butterfly, but it is in fact a moth. It can be found in long grasses on dunes further from the beach.

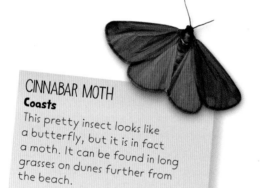

### HEATH SNAIL
**Coasts**
These snails have distinctive stripy shells. But they can still be hard to spot because they're so small – their shell is only about 1cm (0.4 in) across.

## How are dunes formed?
Dunes begin life when wind pushes dry sand into sheltered spots around an obstacle, such as a rock. The dunes grow over time, from small "embryo" dunes to larger mature dunes.

MATURE DUNE

DUNE SLACK

GREY DUNE

YELLOW DUNE

EMBRYO DUNE

FORE DUNE

BEACH

**SCENE SETTER**
The roots of certain grass species hold the sand grains together. This allows other plants to grow there.

# What is sand?

Have you ever wondered exactly what sand is? There are several types of sand and each type is made from something different.

THIS DARK SAND IS MADE OF GROUND UP PIECES OF BLACK VOLCANIC ROCKS.

VOLCANIC SAND

TINY GRAINS OF MINERALS, SUCH AS QUARTZ AND FELDSPAR, MAKE UP THIS SAND.

MINERAL SAND

THIS SAND IS CRACKED PIECES OF BARNACLE AND SNAIL SHELLS.

SHELL SAND

## NATTERJACK TOAD
**Coasts, lakes, wetlands**
This toad is very rare, so it may be hard to find. Its favourite spot is warm, shallow pools in the sand, so keep an eye out for a little toad oasis in the dunes.

YELLOW STRIPE DOWN BACK

## MARRAM GRASS
**Coasts**
Marram grass is well adapted to the windswept dunes. Its stalks are tough and its rolled-up leaves prevent it drying out. It grows golden flowers in the summer.

# WADERS

Wading birds search the soggy sand for food at low tide. Most waders gather in large numbers along the coast when they visit during the winter to feed on the rich supply of burrowing invertebrates.

THE BRIGHT RED BILL MAKES IT EASY TO TELL APART FROM OTHER BIRDS.

### OYSTERCATCHER
**Coasts, grasslands, wetlands**
Listen out for the oystercatcher's loud "peep-peep" calls. They're commonly found on rocky shores, looking for shellfish.

### CURLEW
**Coasts, wetlands**
Curlews are one of the tallest wading birds you'll see on the coast. Their curved bills help them find worms in the sand.

NAMED AFTER THE BLACK RING OF FEATHERS AROUND ITS NECK

### RINGED PLOVER
**Coasts, rivers, wetlands**
Look out for this plover tapping its feet on the sand. This behaviour tricks underground prey into coming out from its hiding place.

## REDSHANK
**Coasts, wetlands**
You might be able to identify this small wading bird even if you're far away, as its bright red legs are easy to spot.

IT HAS A WHITE BAND ON THE BACK OF ITS WINGS.

THE FOUR PURPLE CIRCLES INSIDE MOON JELLYFISH ARE THEIR REPRODUCTIVE ORGANS.

SAND COILS ARE PRODUCED BY LUGWORMS BURROWING BELOW THE SAND.

## PIED AVOCET
**Coasts, rivers, wetlands**
These birds have striking black-and-white markings. They sweep their bill side-to-side in the water to catch prey.

THESE UNUSUAL PACKETS, CALLED "MERMAID'S PURSES", ARE PRODUCED BY SHARKS AND SKATES TO CONTAIN THEIR EGGS.

## BLACK-TAILED GODWIT
**Coasts, grasslands, wetlands**
During breeding season, godwits have ruby-coloured chest feathers. Look out for the black-tipped tail feathers to identify this species.

## On the beach
While you're birdwatching on the beach, make sure you look at the ground too. You might spot weird and wonderful things that give you hints of life out at sea or underground.

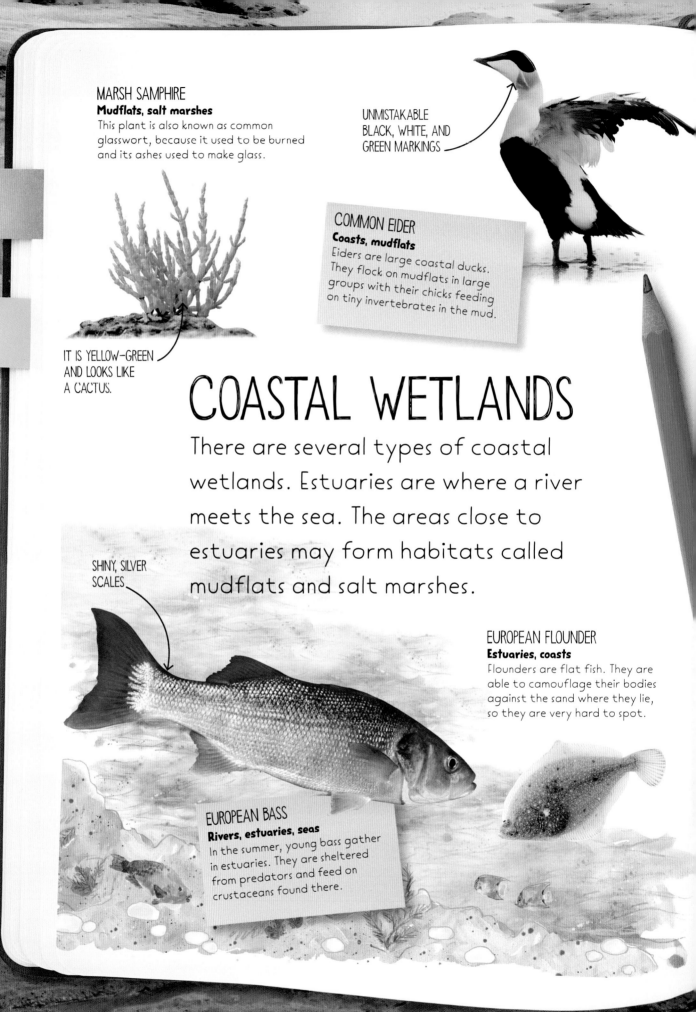

## MARSH SAMPHIRE
**Mudflats, salt marshes**
This plant is also known as common glasswort, because it used to be burned and its ashes used to make glass.

UNMISTAKABLE BLACK, WHITE, AND GREEN MARKINGS

IT IS YELLOW-GREEN AND LOOKS LIKE A CACTUS.

## COMMON EIDER
**Coasts, mudflats**
Eiders are large coastal ducks. They flock on mudflats in large groups with their chicks feeding on tiny invertebrates in the mud.

# COASTAL WETLANDS

There are several types of coastal wetlands. Estuaries are where a river meets the sea. The areas close to estuaries may form habitats called mudflats and salt marshes.

SHINY, SILVER SCALES

## EUROPEAN FLOUNDER
**Estuaries, coasts**
Flounders are flat fish. They are able to camouflage their bodies against the sand where they lie, so they are very hard to spot.

## EUROPEAN BASS
**Rivers, estuaries, seas**
In the summer, young bass gather in estuaries. They are sheltered from predators and feed on crustaceans found there.

## STARWORT MOTH
**Coasts**
Starwort moths are typically brown or beige. Their larvae are green and yellow striped and feed on pink sea aster flowers.

ONE OF THE SMALLEST GEESE, WITH A SMALL HEAD AND VERY SHORT BILL.

## BARNACLE GOOSE
**Salt marshes**
This black-and-white goose grazes on roots and leaves. It migrates from cold northern regions to Europe for a warmer winter.

FLOWERS PROVIDE A SOURCE OF NECTAR FOR BUTTERFLIES.

## SEA ASTER
**Estuaries, salt marshes**
These brightly coloured purple and yellow flowers bloom from July to October.

# Wetlands

Estuaries are large habitats that may contain smaller habitats within them. Some species can only be found in one habitat, while others can be found in more than one.

ESTUARIES ARE THE MEETING POINTS FOR RIVERS AND SEAS. THE WATER VARIES IN SALTINESS DEPENDING ON THE TIDES.

MUD FROM THE RIVER AND SILT FROM THE SEAWATER SETTLE ALONG ESTUARIES TO FORM MUDFLATS.

MUDFLATS BECOME SALT MARSHES WHEN PLANTS BEGIN TO GROW ON THE EXPOSED MUD.

# OFF THE COAST

Marine mammals need to come to the surface to breathe, so you can sometimes spot them from the shore. Keep your eye out for dorsal fins and heads poking out of the waves.

**SCENE SETTER**
For a closer look, ask an adult to find an eco-friendly whale-watching tour. You should still keep your distance in a boat, so you don't disturb the animals.

**ORCA**
**Seas**
This dolphin loves to eat herring and salmon. In summer, it follows the fish as they swim upstream through Norwegian fjords to lay their eggs.

**GREY SEAL**
**Coasts, seas**
Look out for the head of a grey seal breaking the surface of the water as it comes up for air. They can dive for about five minutes at a time.

## Island life

Islands are hard for predators to reach, and they can often have smaller populations of humans. This means islands can be safe havens for animals, such as seals, to raise their young.

**SEA EAGLE**
**Coasts, grasslands, wetlands, forests**
This eagle can be found on many Norwegian islands. It was hunted to extinction in Britain, but has been reintroduced to some Scottish islands.

IT'S MORE COMMON TO SPOT THESE WHALES IN THE SUMMER.

## HUMPBACK WHALE
**Seas**

Whales often jump out of the sea. This is called breaching, and it's not really known why they do it. They might be showing off to other whales.

## LONG-FINNED PILOT WHALE
**Seas**

Look out for this dolphin's long, curved fins breaking the surface of the water. You'll likely see many of them together.

## BASKING SHARK
**Seas**

This giant shark floats close to the sea's surface in calm weather. Look out for its triangular dorsal fin – the pointed fin on its back.

## COMMON SEAL
**Coasts, seas**

Common seals come onto the shores of the Outer Hebrides in Scotland to breed. Listen out for their distinctive, dog-like bark – but don't get too close.

## MANX SHEARWATER
**Coasts**

Half of all Manx shearwaters nest at night on Skomer Island in Wales. The best time to see them is late spring, as they migrate to South America for the rest of the year.

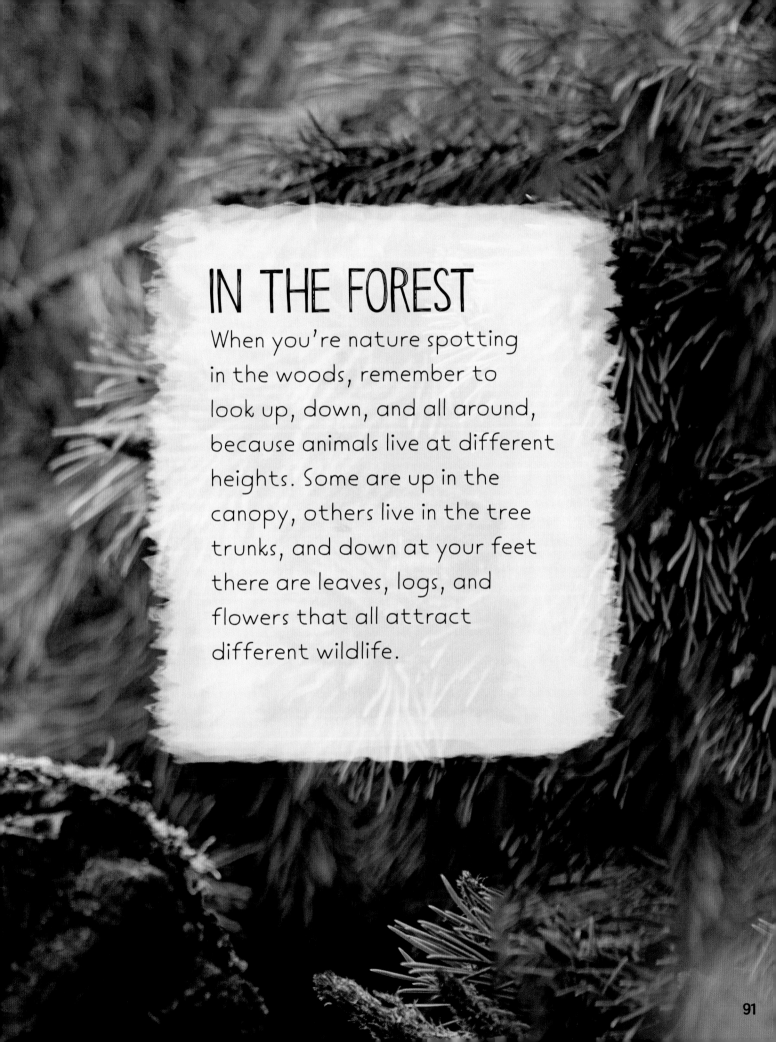

# IN THE FOREST

When you're nature spotting in the woods, remember to look up, down, and all around, because animals live at different heights. Some are up in the canopy, others live in the tree trunks, and down at your feet there are leaves, logs, and flowers that all attract different wildlife.

# FOREST LIVING

In forests, some animals live high up in the trees. The leafy canopy creates shaded, sheltered ground below, providing homes for all sorts of wildlife.

## Human impact

As the human population grows, woodlands are cut down to make space for people to live and grow food. This is called deforestation.

THE EURASIAN LYNX IS AN ENDANGERED SPECIES.

### LIFE AT RISK
Deforestation means that the animals who rely on this habitat have less space to find shelter and food. Some species have become endangered.

## Forests in danger

Pollution we emit into the atmosphere can cause acid rain. This damages leaves, and removes important nutrients from forest soil.

### CLIMATE CHANGE
Climate change can lead to drastic weather, such as heat waves that can cause wildfires. Rising temperatures can also affect migration, and the times when plants flower.

## Forest growth

A forest does not appear overnight. It takes years, sometimes centuries, before tiny seedlings grow into tall, majestic trees.

# Helping woodlands

It's important to protect our forests and their biodiversity. Even your local woodlands may be in need of help.

## GET EDUCATED

There are lots of organizations and trusts that work to teach us about our forests. Find out about the groups that work with your local woodlands.

## GET INVOLVED

Some organizations need volunteers to help them in their work. Ask an adult to help you research ways you can help your local forests.

# ALL ABOUT TREES

There are two main types of forests. Deciduous forests are mainly made up of trees that lose their leaves in winter. In evergreen forests, most trees keep their leaves all year round.

### COMMON ALDER
**Forests, wetlands**

Alders are deciduous, water-loving trees, so you're likely to find them next to rivers. Their yellow flowers bloom in the spring.

DECIDUOUS: WIDE, BROAD-LEAVED

EVERGREEN: THIN, CONIFEROUS

## Know your trees

Normally, deciduous trees are wide and have broad leaves. Evergreen trees are usually thin and coniferous – they have cones and needle-like leaves.

### HORNBEAM
**Forests**

These large, deciduous trees can grow up to 30 m (98 ft) tall. Hornbeams are often found in Europe's most ancient woodlands.

LEAVES TURN GOLD IN AUTUMN.

### FIELD MAPLE
**Forests**

These small, deciduous trees are normally dark green. They stand out a lot more in autumn when they turn a yellow-gold colour.

## SCENE SETTER
Forests managed by woodland trusts and national parks have the most types of trees. Rangers look after them to make sure they're healthy.

## SCOTS PINE
**Forests, heathlands**
These impressive evergreen trees are only found in Scotland. The patchy bark lower on the trunk looks like scales.

## JUNIPER
**Forests, grasslands, heathlands**
Junipers are evergreen coniferous trees. Their leaves are thin and needle-like, and their cones look like blueberries.

JUNIPER BERRIES ARE POISONOUS — DON'T EAT THEM!

## NORWAY SPRUCE
**Forests, mountains**
This coniferous tree is native to Scandinavia. It can live for over 1,000 years! Norway spruces are often used as Christmas trees.

### Top tip
WHILE YOU'RE ENJOYING IDENTIFYING THE TREES AROUND YOU, DON'T FORGET TO LOOK UP. THERE MIGHT BE ANIMALS IN THE CANOPY.

**JAY**
**Forests, grasslands**
Jays are colourful relatives of crows. They collect the oak's acorns and bury them in autumn so they can eat them in the winter.

**BECHSTEIN'S BAT**
**Forests, grasslands**
These bats are quite rare, so they may be hard to find. You're most likely to see their nesting spots: dips in oak trunk bark.

SQUIRRELS GATHER TWIGS AND BARK TO MAKE THEIR NESTS.

**ROE DEER**
**Forests, grasslands**
Roe deer graze on oak saplings and leaves. Females don't have antlers. Tread quietly if you see a deer, as they are easily spooked.

# JUST ONE TREE

A single tree can support all kinds of life, both big and small. The European oak can support more wildlife than most, because its wind-pollinated flowers produce a yearly crop of acorns that animals love to eat.

### COMMON OAK
**Forests**
Oaks can live for over 500 years. In that time, they sprout nuts called acorns, which some animals eat.

### CATERPILLAR
**Forests**
Caterpillars of the purple hairstreak butterfly are flat and brown coloured. They feast on the flower buds and leaves of oak trees.

### EURASIAN BADGER
**Forests, grasslands**
Badgers love to shuffle in the leaf litter under oaks, searching for tasty acorns to eat.

### MILK-CAP
**Forests**
This species of fungi has a "mycorrhizal" relationship with oak trees: they help provide each other with extra moisture and nutrients.

## Moth magnet
Moths like a sweet treat almost as much as you do! Mix a bit of honey or jam with water and spread it on a tree trunk. Come back later and you'll find moths have flocked to this sugary snack.

USE A PAINT BRUSH TO SPREAD THE PASTE ONTO THE TRUNK WHEN IT'S GETTING DARK.

THE SWEET SMELL WILL ATTRACT MOTHS. CHECK BACK LATER WITH A TORCH.

# UNDER THE TREES

The forest floor is a varied mini-habitat. Dense plants provide shelter, fallen branches and fruit offer food, and the soils are fertile places for plants and fungi to grow.

## HARVESTMAN
**Forests**
Harvestmen are arachnids that are closely related to spiders. Their body is not separated, like a spider's is, and they only have one pair of eyes.

## LEMON SLUG
**Forests**
To see these slimy slugs feasting on fungi, you'll need to go to very old woodland - they're often found in protected national parks.

## MALE FERN
**Forests, towns**
In the spring, this fern's scaly, brown stems steadily uncurl. By the summer, its lush green fern fronds have spread out.

## BANK VOLE
**Forests, grasslands**
Bank voles aren't fussy eaters. They can be found rooting around in the leaf litter for insects, roots, fungi, fruit, and nuts.

## Amazing acorns

Every few years, some oaks produce almost no acorns. The next year, they'll make up the loss by producing thousands! This is called a "mast year".

### RING-NECKED PHEASANT
**Forests**
Male pheasants have amber-coloured plumage and blue-green heads. Female pheasants are mottled brown.

### SOUTHERN WOOD ANT
**Forests**
If you spot a large colony of ants around a nest, make sure to keep your distance. They may spray acid to defend themselves.

ACORNS PROVIDE FOOD FOR MANY ANIMALS.

### CHANTERELLE MUSHROOM
**Forests**
These yellow or orange mushrooms can be found in mossy patches in forests. They sometimes smell fruity, like apricots.

### COMMON POLYPODY
**Forests, heathlands**
This species is a deeper green colour than male ferns. Small capsules under their leaves send out spores (tiny cells), which then grow into new ferns.

99

# ON A LOG

Dead wood can be buzzing with activity, so fallen logs are a great place for nature spotters to investigate. Here insects and fungi feed on dead wood. Animals higher up the food chain visit rotting logs to hunt for insects.

## WASP BEETLE
**Forests, grasslands**
Similar to stag beetles, these insects lay their eggs in rotting wood. Look out for them near beech and ash trees.

## OYSTER MUSHROOM
**Forests**
These fungi are often found on beechwood and oak stumps, using nutrients from dead and dying wood.

## STAG BEETLE
**Forests**
Female stag beetles seek out logs to lay their eggs. Once they hatch, the larvae feast on the nutrient-filled wood.

## COMMON EARTHWORM
**Forests, towns**
Earthworms pull leaves into their burrows to eat, then poo them out. This releases important nutrients back into the soil.

## COMMON TAMARISK MOSS
**Forests**
These beautiful, bright-green mosses grow on moist logs, giving the forest floor a dash of colour. Their shoots look like tiny ferns.

# Log visitors

On the hunt for food, some birds and mammals will often stop by logs to feast on the bounty of insects that live there.

COMMON SHREWS NEED TO EAT A LOT, SO THEY VISIT LOGS FOR A FEAST.

BADGERS HAVE A VARIED DIET, SO LOGS OFFER PLENTY OF CHOICES.

## WOODLOUSE SPIDER
**Forests**
Look out for this spider's silky web in the nooks and crevices of logs. Its pale body and red legs make it easy to spot.

## COMMON CENTIPEDE
**Forests, grasslands**
Centipedes don't really like the daylight – they hide in dark parts of logs, then come out at night to scuttle about.

# IN A CLEARING

Plants need sunlight to make food, so lots of forest flowers grow in clearings, where there are fewer trees to block the light. The colourful flowers also attract pollinators.

## WILD GARLIC
**Forests**
The flowers of wild garlic are very small, white, and pin-like. This is different from the garlic that's used for cooking.

## BLUEBELL
**Forests, grasslands**
You know you're in ancient woodland if you see bluebells. They often grow in densely-packed carpets along the forest floor.

## LILY-OF-THE-VALLEY
**Forests, grasslands**
These late summer bloomers are common throughout much of Europe. Despite its name, this is a member of the asparagus family!

WHITE, BELL-SHAPED
FLOWERS DROOP
DOWNWARDS

## COMMON WOOD SORREL
**Forests**
Wood sorrel doesn't mind the shade, and can survive growing on the forest floor underneath thick leaf cover.

## Bursting into bloom

Most flowers will bloom in the spring months of April and May. However, some flowers bloom earlier, in March, to take advantage of direct sunlight before trees regain their leaves and create more shade.

### WOOD ANEMONE
**Forests, towns**
Wood anemone are some of the first flowers to bloom in the spring. You can spot them as early as March.

### FOXGLOVE
**Forests**
Foxglove flowers are a vivid purple-pink. They attract bees that have especially long tongues that can reach inside.

## Insects

You can spot all kinds of insects visiting flowers in forests. They come to feed on the flowers' nectar, but they also work as pollinators and help the flowers to spread their pollen.

### BROAD-BORDERED BEE HAWK-MOTH
**Forests**
In northern Europe, look out for these big moths in sunny forest glades during the day. They're summer-loving creatures.

### THICK-LEGGED FLOWER BEETLE
**Forests, towns, grasslands**
You might spot these beetles thanks to sunlight glinting off their shiny bodies as they pollinate flowers.

### COMMON BANDED HOVERFLY
**Forests**
This insect visits foxglove flowers. It's easiest to spot in the spring and summer months.

## TAWNY OWL
**Forests, towns, grasslands**
This owl sits patiently on a perch, then swoops down on unsuspecting prey. Listen out for its "too-wit too-woo" calls at night.

## SCENE SETTER
Top predators are rare sightings. They have large hunting ranges, so their populations are very spaced out.

# WOODLAND HUNTERS

Bushes, trees, and dense undergrowth provide the perfect cover for prey. Forest predators must be skilled hunters to succeed.

## EURASIAN LYNX
**Forests, grasslands**
In northern Europe, the lynx can only be spotted in Scandinavia and Germany. It can take down animals that are bigger than itself.

### SPARROWHAWK
**Forests, grasslands**
Sparrowhawks are agile fliers, which helps them chase their prey through all the obstacles of a tree-filled forest.

### COMMON SHREW
**Forests, grasslands**
This tiny mammal looks like a long-nosed mouse. It scurries quickly, searching for worms. It must eat every few hours to survive.

THESE SHREWS SQUEAK LOUDLY WHEN THEY FIGHT FOR THEIR TERRITORY.

### STONE MARTEN
**Forests, towns, mountains**
The stone marten is only found in mainland Europe. You can tell it apart from a weasel because it is about four times bigger.

# Hungry hunters

There may be lots of places for animals to hide in the forest, but these predators have clever tactics to help them catch their prey.

SPARROWHAWKS GIVE CHASE, ZIPPING BETWEEN BRANCHES TO CATCH BIRDS.

WEASELS ARE AGILE, AND CAN WRAP THEIR BODIES AROUND PREY.

LYNXES LIE IN WAIT TO AMBUSH PREY.

## OAK BRACKET
**Forests**
This fungus can be found on both live and dead trees. It gives out a thick amber liquid that looks like honey.

## BEECHWOOD SICKENER
**Forests**
This fungus helps the beech tree where it lives to take up nutrients from the soil. It's quite small, only around 4 cm (1.5 in) tall.

# FOREST FUNGI

Fungi connect to tree roots to use the tree's nutrients and moisture. What you see above ground are the "fruits" – most of their bodies grow underground!

## PENNY BUN
**Forests, grasslands**
The penny bun is quite a common mushroom in Europe. It is eaten by many animals.

THE DEATHCAP IS THE MOST TOXIC OF ALL. IT LOOKS VERY SIMILAR TO THE HARMLESS FIELD MUSHROOM.

## Keep clear!
You might love mushrooms on your dinner plate, but you must never eat them from the ground, no matter how colourful they are. Some are very poisonous and dangerous to humans.

## TRUFFLE
**Forests**
This is the most common species of truffle in Europe. It grows underground on beech tree roots.

## STUMP PUFFBALL
**Forests**
Stump puffballs are unusual for fungi – they don't have a distinct stem (the long stalk) and cap (the top).

SMOOTH APPEARANCE

## BROWN ROLL-RIM
**Forests, towns**
These look similar to edible mushrooms, but they're poisonous. They are usually brown, but can also have shades of yellow.

## FLY AGARIC
**Forests, heathlands**
Fly agaric are easy to spot with their red-and-white caps. They can grow quite tall, reaching about 40 cm (16 in).

PEOPLE ONCE BELIEVED FAIRIES LIVED UNDER FLY AGARIC.

# TAIGA FORESTS

Taiga are forests made up of coniferous trees, such as spruce and larch. They are also called boreal forests. The wildlife here needs to withstand regular snowfall and freezing temperatures.

## EURASIAN THREE-TOED WOODPECKER
**Forests**
This woodpecker eats insects that live in dead wood. It can be found in patches of forest where the trees have been killed off by fire or disease.

## HAWK OWL
**Forests, grasslands, wetlands**
You're most likely to see hawk owls out and about in the day. They perch in clearings, keeping an eye out for voles.

## EUROPEAN LARCH
**Forests**
Expect to see these trees everywhere you look. They lose their leaves in winter, unlike most other trees found in the taiga.

## BROWN BEAR
**Forests**
These animals used to be common all over Europe. Now, there are few of them.

## Protecting taiga

Taiga are some of the most ancient forests in Europe. Wolves and bears were once hunted to extinction in these forests, but they have now been reintroduced.

IN NORTHERN EUROPE, TAIGA FORESTS ARE FOUND IN SCOTLAND AND NORWAY.

### SIBERIAN JAY
**Forests**
These birds nest in the dense cover of spruce or pine trees, where they can hide from predators. They use twigs to build their nests, though they sometimes use reindeer hair, too!

### Top tip
YOUR BEST CHANCE TO SPOT BEARS AND WOLVES IS A SUMMER VISIT TO THE TAIGA OF KAINUU, IN FINLAND. GO WITH A GUIDE, AND NEVER APPROACH THE ANIMALS.

### PINE GROSBEAK
**Forests**
Pine grosbeaks have a sweet tooth – you'll find them feasting on juicy red berries that sprout on various taiga trees.

### GREY WOLF
**Forests**
There are only 12,000 wolves in Europe. Highly social animals, they hunt in packs and have huge territories.

WOLVES WERE HUNTED TO EXTINCTION IN SOME NORTHERN EUROPEAN COUNTRIES.

# ON HIGH GROUND

Mountains are some of the most challenging habitats for both wildlife and nature spotters. Plants and animals need to be tough to survive the wild weather and freezing temperatures. People also need to put in a lot of effort to reach these remote locations and spot some rare, exciting species.

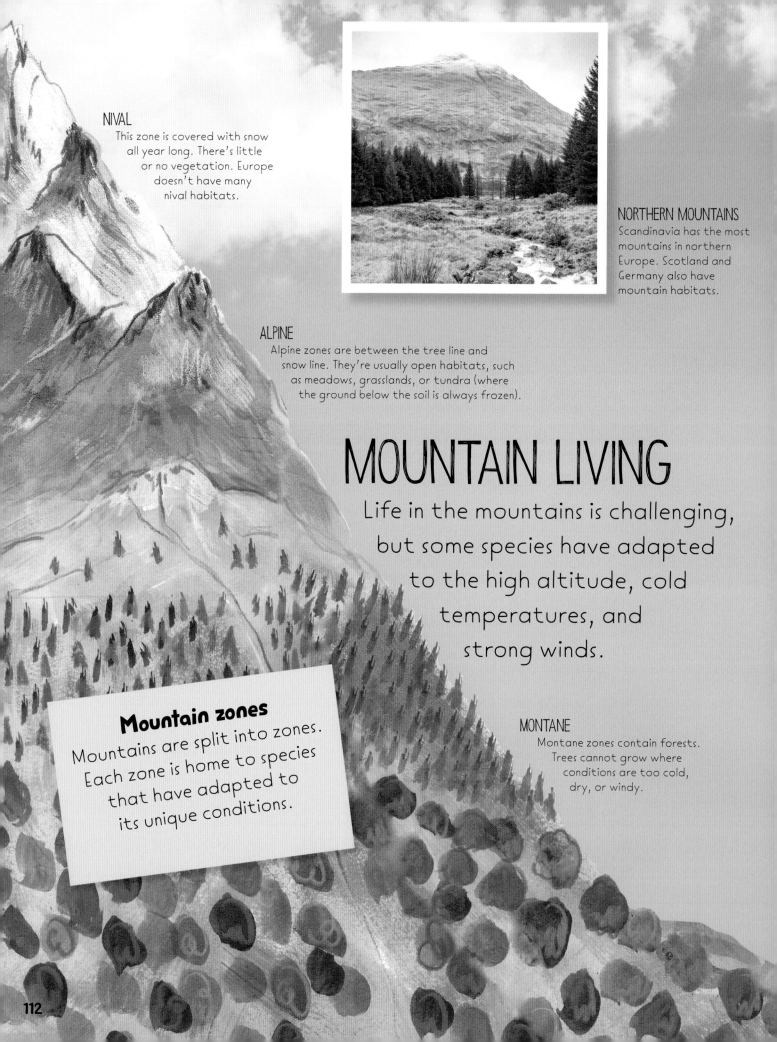

### NIVAL
This zone is covered with snow all year long. There's little or no vegetation. Europe doesn't have many nival habitats.

### NORTHERN MOUNTAINS
Scandinavia has the most mountains in northern Europe. Scotland and Germany also have mountain habitats.

### ALPINE
Alpine zones are between the tree line and snow line. They're usually open habitats, such as meadows, grasslands, or tundra (where the ground below the soil is always frozen).

# MOUNTAIN LIVING
Life in the mountains is challenging, but some species have adapted to the high altitude, cold temperatures, and strong winds.

### Mountain zones
Mountains are split into zones. Each zone is home to species that have adapted to its unique conditions.

### MONTANE
Montane zones contain forests. Trees cannot grow where conditions are too cold, dry, or windy.

## Adaptation

Mountains get colder as you go higher up. There's also plenty of wind and rain. Wildlife has had to adapt to survive these harsh conditions.

**BRILLIANT BIRDS**
Ptarmigan are white so that they are camouflaged against the snow. This helps them hide from predators.

FLOWERS ONLY OPEN WHEN IT'S SUNNY

**PLANT POWER**
The alpine gentian can survive harsh, dry mountain conditions because it has deep roots to absorb as much water as possible.

## In the mountains

Mountains are undisturbed compared to other habitats, because they're not suitable for farms or big towns. However, humans have still had an impact on mountain habitats.

**BE CAREFUL**
Mountains are hard to reach and dangerous to explore. Always go with an adult, stick to the trail, and wear suitable clothing.

**SKI RESORTS**
Mountain animals are naturally shy and wary of humans as people are so uncommon in their habitat. You might not see much wildlife close to busy ski resorts.

# HIGHLAND FORESTS

Mountain forests are usually made up of coniferous trees, many of which stay green all year. Plants and animals that live in these forests must be able to handle snow.

## WESTERN CAPERCAILLIE
**Forests**
In April, male capercaillies will puff out their chests and make whistling noises to attract mates. This behaviour is called "lekking".

## PINE MARTEN
**Forests**
The nocturnal pine marten is hard to spot. Instead, look for its blue or red tinged poo – the colour depends on the berries the marten eats.

### COMMON GOLDENEYE
**Forests, rivers, wetlands**
These ducks nest up in coniferous trees, safe from predators. They're often found in trees close to rivers and lakes.

THE COMMON GOLDENEYE LIKES TO NEST IN TREE HOLES.

### WILDCAT
**Forests**
The wildcat is endangered and rare. During winter, when food is hard to find, it might try to hunt much bigger prey, such as deer.

## Pine cones
Coniferous trees produce their seeds in wooden structures called cones. The cones split open, then the wind scatters the seeds. Many forest animals rely on these seeds for food.

IT HAS A SPECIALIZED BILL TO EXTRACT CONE SEEDS.

### SCOTTISH CROSSBILL
**Forests**
This bird feeds on the seeds from cones. It is the only species of bird found in the British Isles and nowhere else in the world.

ITS EAR TUFTS ARE LONGER IN THE WINTER.

### EURASIAN RED SQUIRREL
**Forests**
Red squirrels are messy eaters, leaving empty cores behind after they have feasted on pine cones.

THIS TIT STORES SEEDS FOR THE WINTER.

### CRESTED TIT
**Forests**
You're most likely to spot this bird after the spring breeding season, when it gathers in groups with other small birds.

115

# ALPINE MEADOWS

Alpine meadows are found high in the mountains, above the trees. They are some of the most pretty, untouched habitats, so if you can get to them, they're well worth the journey.

## MEADOW PIPIT
**Mountains, wetlands**
Pipits feed on insects and seeds. Their nests are surprisingly neat – made of grass and hair, usually in hidden nooks.

## DARK-BORDERED BEAUTY MOTH
**Mountains**
Dark-bordered beauty moths are well camouflaged against autumn leaf litter. You can spot it flying around at sunrise and sunset.

ITS WING COLOURS HIDE THIS MOTH AGAINST BROWN AUTUMN LEAVES.

## MOUNTAIN RINGLET
**Mountains**
Mountain ringlets only come out when the sun is shining. On cloudy days, they hide in thick tussock grass.

## ALPINE SAW-WORT
**Mountains, forests**
Alpine saw-worts are descended from plants that lived through the Ice Age, so it's pretty tough!

## EARLY-PURPLE ORCHID
**Mountains, forests**
This is one of the first alpine flowers to bloom in the spring. It smells sweet when it first opens, but then it starts to stink!

### RING OUZEL
**Mountains, forests**
This bird doesn't live in alpine meadows all year round. It spends the winter in warmer places, such as the Mediterranean.

# Sheltering for winter
Plants need to be tough to survive life in the mountains. They need to withstand strong winds and heavy snowfall, and also grow on bare rocks with little soil.

GLACIER CROWFOOT CAN GROW ON GROUND THAT IS DAMP FROM SNOW.

### GLACIER CROWFOOT
**Mountains, tundra**
Glacier crowfoot flowers are a protected species in Finland. They bloom on mountain meadows but also on icy tundra above the Arctic Circle.

### SCABIOUS MINING BEE
**Mountains, coasts, forests**
These bees take to the skies between July and September. They rely on scabious – a type of plant that produces lots of nectar.

### ALPINE MARMOT
**Mountains**
Marmots graze on grasses and herbs, like mini-cows. Huge colonies of them live in vast underground burrows.

### ALPINE MILK-VETCH
**Mountains, grasslands**
The spindly alpine milk-vetch might look fragile, but they can withstand temperatures below freezing.

# HIGH HUNTERS

Mountainous areas can be good for spotting birds of prey. In these habitats, the birds can fly high over the wide, open landscape to hunt for prey.

SPOTTED PLUMAGE

## GYRFALCON
**Mountains, forests, tundra**
Gyrfalcons are the largest type of falcon. They are super fast fliers, reaching speeds of up to 105 kph (65mph).

BIRDS WITH SHORT, POINTED WINGS CAN FLY FASTEST.

## PEREGRINE FALCON
**Mountains, towns, wetlands**
Peregrine falcons are the fastest animals on the planet. They can dive at speeds of up to 320 kph (200 mph)!

HUGE WINGSPAN OF OVER 2 M (6.5 FT)

## GOLDEN EAGLE
**Mountains**
Golden eagles mate for life. They have large territories. Younger eagles have white patches on their wings and tails.

BIGGER THAN MOST OTHER BIRDS OF PREY

CREAM-COLOURED HEAD AND UNDERWING

## ROUGH-LEGGED BUZZARD
**Mountains, wetlands**
You can identify a rough-legged buzzard by the feathers that go all the way down its legs. This is uncommon in birds of prey.

# Prey animals
These birds may be great hunters, but their prey have evolved ways to avoid being caught.

## NORWAY BROWN LEMMING
**Mountains**
These rodents stay in the safety of their burrows and rocks to avoid being seen.

## ROCK DOVE
**Mountains, towns**
These doves gather in large flocks to make it difficult for falcons to single them out.

## MOUNTAIN HARE
**Mountains**
Hares are super-speedy runners, zig-zagging across the mountains to avoid capture.

119

# BETWEEN THE CRACKS

Not all plants need grassy ground to survive. Some mountain plants have long roots that extend into cracks and crevices. Others attach themselves to the rock itself.

## ALPINE LADY-FERN
**Mountains**
Alpine lady-ferns grow in Scandinavian fjords. They even survive in some of the harsh, volcanic rock environments of Iceland.

## CURVED WOOD-RUSH
**Mountains**
Curved wood-rush is found only in northern Europe. It's very short, and only grows to about 10-20 cm (4-8 in) to stay out of the wind.

## HIGHLAND SAXIFRAGE
**Mountains**
This plant mainly grows in the Arctic and is rarer further south, but you can find it growing in damp rocky spots in the Scottish Highlands.

## Nesting birds
These birds have also adapted to life in the craggy mountainside. Rocks can be great places to build hidden nests and shelter out of reach from predators.

## EURASIAN DOTTEREL
**Mountains**
The dotterel makes an annual journey from northern Africa to the north of Scandinavia.

IT HAS A CHESTNUT-COLOURED BREAST IN SUMMER.

## Alpine garden

Alpine gardens are easy to take care of. Just watch out for the water level – if the soil stays too soggy, the plants will die. A hole in the bottom of the pot will help the water to drain away.

STEP 1: GET A STONE POT AND CHOOSE SOME PLANTS.

STEP 2: ADD SOIL, SAND, GRIT, COMPOST, AND ROCKS.

STEP 3: PLANT THE ALPINE PLANTS.

STEP 4: MAKE SURE THEY DON'T GET TOO SOGGY.

### HIGHLAND CUDWEED
**Mountains**

Highland cudweed has surprisingly hairy leaves. This makes the surface area of the leaves bigger, helping the plant keep moisture in.

### PARSLEY FERN
**Mountains**

This plant looks a lot like parsley, which we use in cooking. It only grows where there is no trace of lime (a mineral) in the rocks.

### ROCK PTARMIGAN
**Mountains**

In the winter months, ptarmigan plumage becomes completely white to camouflage them against the snow.

THIS BIRD STILL HAS A FEW OF ITS DARK SUMMER FEATHERS.

### ALPINE CHOUGH
**Mountains**

These birds are found in the Alps. Pairs of chough live life on the edge – they nest on cliff faces. The chough is a bird in the crow family, but unlike crows, it has a yellow bill instead of a black bill.

YELLOW BILL

# MOUNTAIN TUNDRA

Tundra is found in the mountains and in the far north where it's very cold. A layer of permafrost keeps the ground frozen all year.

BOTH MALES AND FEMALES GROW ANTLERS.

## DWARF BIRCH
**Tundra**
These plants are very important in the tundra because they feed grazing animals, such as reindeer.

## REINDEER
**Tundra, grasslands, forests**
Reindeer spend summer in the open tundra, munching on the growing plants. In the winter, they move to taiga forests.

## NORTHERN WOLF'S-BANE
**Tundra**
This plant got its name from farmers in medieval times, who used it to poison wolves that ate their livestock.

## REINDEER LICHEN
**Tundra**
Reindeer lichen are able to absorb water through the air – this helps them to survive in tundra when the groundwater has frozen.

## WOLVERINE
**Tundra, grasslands, forests**
Wolverines are fierce predators that can take down much bigger prey. They are solitary, spending most of their time alone.

## CLOUDBERRY
**Tundra, woods**
Cloudberries bring a dash of vivid red to the tundra during the summer months, from June to August.

## SCURFY DECEIVER
**Tundra, grasslands, forests**
The scurfy deceiver thrives in acidic soils often found in Arctic environments. It tends to grow near pine trees.

## WILLOW PTARMIGAN
**Tundra**
These birds don't always need to fly over this difficult terrain. They can also walk in deep snow with their feathered feet.

## BEARBERRY
**Tundra**
Bearberry flowers are an important source of nectar for mountain insects. The berries offer nutritious, sweet treats for bears.

## Changing colours
Many animals that live all year in the tundra turn white for winter. This lets them hide against the snow, hopefully staying hidden from their predators or prey.

THIS ARCTIC FOX HAS ITS WHITE WINTER COAT.

## GOAT WILLOW
**Tundra, grasslands, forests**
Goat willow has furry, paw-like catkins that grow close to the ground. This helps to protect them from being damaged by ice and frost.

## ARCTIC FOX
**Tundra**
These foxes survive in the tundra by building underground dens, where they can hide from harsh weather.

# GLOSSARY

**Adapt** How a living thing changes its appearance or behaviour to better fit in with its environment

**Alpine** The area of a mountain between the tree line and snow line

**Altitude** How high above sea-level or the ground something is

**Amphibian** Cold-blooded vertebrates that start life in water before moving between land and water when fully grown

**Aquatic** Found in the water

**Artificial** Made by humans

**Bill** Jaws of a bird

**Biodiversity** The variety of plants and animals that live in an area

**Birds** Warm-blooded vertebrates with feathers; can usually fly

**Camouflage** Colours or patterns on an animal's skin, fur, or feathers that help it blend in with its environment

**Carnivore** Animal that eats meat

**Climate** The weather that is usual for an area over a long period of time

**Climate change** Change in temperature and weather across the Earth that can be natural or caused by human activity

**Cold-blooded** Animals whose body temperature changes with the environment

**Coniferous** Type of evergreen tree, usually with needle-like leaves

**Conservation** Protecting environments and wildlife

**Crepuscular** Active at twilight

**Crustacean** An invertebrate with jointed legs and often a hard shell or exoskeleton, such as a crab, shrimp, or woodlouse

**Dabbling** The way some waterfowl upend in the water to feed on aquatic food with their heads under the surface and bottom in the air

**Dam** A barrier that holds back water

**Deciduous** A plant that loses all its leaves in the winter

**Deforestation** Cutting down trees and destroying forests

**Diurnal** Active during the day time

**Dorsal fin** A fin on the back of some aquatic animals

**Ecosystem** A community of living things and their non-living environment – including the soil, water, and air around them

**Erosion** Gradual wearing away of rocks due to water and weather

**Estuary** End of a river where freshwater meets the sea

**Fauna** Animals

**Fish** Cold-blooded vertebrates that live underwater and have scales

**Flooding** When a river or the sea overflows and fills land with water

**Flora** Plants

**Forage** When animals search for food

**Fungi** Group of living things, including mushrooms and moulds, that break down dead plants and animals to obtain food

**Germinate** When a seed starts to grow

**Habitat** Area where an animal or plant lives

**Herbivore** Animal that eats only plant matter

**Hibernation** Period of inactivity that some animals go through in the winter

**High tide** When the sea level is at its highest

**Insect** Type of invertebrate with six legs and a three-part body

**Intertidal zone** An area of the shore that is covered by water at high tide, and uncovered at low tide

**Invertebrate** Animals that do not have a spinal column, such as insects, worms, jellyfish, and spiders

**Larva** Young of certain kinds of animals that look very different from their adult forms

**Low tide** When the sea level is at its lowest

**Mammal** Vertebrate animal that is fed by milk from its mother when it is young

**Marine** Found in the sea

**Migration** Seasonal or periodic movement by animals from one region to another

**Mycorrhizae** Underground fibres of fungi that grow around tree roots and help the trees draw nutrients from the ground

**Native** Species that have always lived in an area, rather than being introduced

**Nocturnal** Active at night

**Omnivore** Animal that eats both plants and meat

**Permafrost** A layer of permanently frozen soil underground

**Pest** Animal that attacks or destroys things, such as crops

**Plumage** All of a bird's feathers

**Poisonous** Something that causes harm if eaten or touched

**Pollen** Powder that comes from flowering plants and is used in pollination

**Pollination** Transfer of pollen from one plant to another so those plants can reproduce

**Pollinator** Animals that help plants to spread pollen

**Pollution** Harmful substances in the air, soil, or water

**Predator** Animal that hunts other living animals for food

**Prey** Animal that is hunted by another animal for food

**Reptile** Cold-blooded vertebrate with scaly skin that usually reproduces by laying eggs

**Scavenger** Animal that feeds on the remains of dead animals

**Sexual dimorphism** When male and female animals of the same species look different

**Shed** When an animal or plant loses part of its external body, such as skin or fur

**Species** Specific types of animals or plants with shared features that can mate and produce young together

**Territory** The area that an animal considers its own and that it will defend from other animals

**Tundra** A cold, treeless area where soil remains frozen

**Urban** A built-up area, such as a city or a large town

**Venomous** Substance that may be deadly if injected by an animal or plant, through a sting or fangs

**Vertebrate** Animals having a backbone or spine and a brain enclosed within a skull, such as mammals and birds

**Warm-blooded** Animal that keeps a constant body temperature

**Wetlands** Areas of land that are flooded with water, either temporarily or permanently

# INDEX

# ACKNOWLEDGEMENTS

The publisher would like to thank the following for their kind permission to reproduce their photographs:(Key: a-above; b-below/bottom; c-centre; f-far; l-left; r-right; t-top)
**1 Dreamstime.com:** Goncharov Evgenii (cb). **2 Alamy Stock Photo:** Frank Hecker (tr). **3 123RF.com:** lanwool (crb). **Dreamstime.com:** David Head (cr); Tommason (br). **4-5 Dreamstime.com:** Ksushsh (cb); Roman Novitskii (b). **4 Alamy Stock Photo:** Nature Picture Library (cr). **5 Dreamstime.com:** Robert Kneschke (c). **Getty Images / iStock:** SolStock (tl). **6 Alamy Stock Photo:** Dominic Robinson (tr). **Dreamstime.com:** Christian Schmalhofer (clb); Tommason (tl, crb). **6-7 Dreamstime.com:** Roman Novitskii. **7 123RF.com:** Vitalii Gulay / Vitalisg (tl). **Alamy Stock Photo:** Clement Philippe / Arterra Picture Library (cla). **Dreamstime.com:** Tommason (ftr). **Getty Images:** Arterra / Universal Images Group (tr); Morgan Stephenson (clb). **Getty Images / iStock:** Malerapaso (fcr); technotr (c). **8 Alamy Stock Photo:** Acorn 1 (tr); Franz Christoph Robiller / imageBROKER (c). **Dreamstime.com:** Denys Kuvaiev (br). **Getty Images / iStock:** Andrew_Howe (cl). **8-9 Dreamstime.com:** Spinkly. **9 Alamy Stock Photo:** Craig Joiner Photography (clb). **Dreamstime.com:** Naturefriend (cra). **Getty Images / iStock:** Milan Krasula (crb); Mauinow1 (cl). **10 123RF.com:** Koosen (bc). **Alamy Stock Photo:** Garry Bowden (cr). **Getty Images:** Lane Oatey / Blue Jean Images (ca). **10-11 Dreamstime.com:** Roman Novitskii (b). **Getty Images / iStock:** AmArtPhotography (t). **11 Alamy Stock Photo:** Coyote-Photography.co.uk (cl). **Dreamstime.com:** Catalin205 (clb). **12 Dreamstime.com:** Rangizzz (t); Tommason (br). **12-13 Alamy Stock Photo:** Oleksandr Sokolenko (Background). **Dreamstime.com:** Jon Bilous. **13 Dreamstime.com:** Rudolf Ernst (tl). **Getty Images / iStock:** FatCamera (crb). **14 Alamy Stock Photo:** Stephen Dalton / Avalon / Photoshot License (tc). **Dreamstime.com:** Javier Alonso Huerta (cra). **Getty Images:** Mikroman6 (crb). **14-15 Dreamstime.com:** MNStudio. **15 Alamy Stock Photo:** Tim Gainey (cla); Alan Novelli (tl). **16-17 Alamy Stock Photo:** Dominic Robinson. **18 Alamy Stock Photo:** Anthony David Baynes (tc); Realimage (clb). **Dreamstime.com:** Christinlola (cb). **19 Alamy Stock Photo:** Ian Hubball (tl); Pat Tuson (c); Laurent Geslin / Nature Picture Library (clb). **Dreamstime.com:** Vasyl Helevachuk (bl). **20 Dreamstime.com:** Stuartan (bc). **20-21 Dreamstime.com:** Votchitsev Viacheslav / Imaster (b); Sutichak (c); Roman Novitskii (cb). **21 Alamy Stock Photo:** Agami / Ran Schols / AGAMI Photo Agency (tc). **Dorling Kindersley:** Chris Gomersall Photography (c). **Dreamstime.com:** Helen Davies (bl); Sataporn Jiwjalaen / Onairjiw (r). **22-23 Getty Images / iStock:** Duncan1890. **22 Depositphotos Inc:** Brazil (crb). **Dreamstime.com:** Fosterss (fcl); Javier Alonso Huerta (cr). **Getty Images / iStock:** Leopardinatree (cl). **23 Dreamstime.com:** Agami Photo Agency (tl); Agdbeukhof (ca); Slowmotiongli (cr); Anmbph (cb); Alexander Potapov (crb), Isselee (clb), Elena Schweitzer (cb/mealworms). **Getty Images / iStock:** Elmvilla (ca/garden feeder). **24 Alamy Stock Photo:** Colin Varndell (cl). **Depositphotos Inc:** Ohmega1982 (t). **Dreamstime.com:** Cynoclub (br); Rudmer Zwerver (cla); Tommason (bl, fbr). **24-25 Dreamstime.com:** Andrey Khokhlov. **25 Alamy Stock Photo:** FLPA (tr). **Dreamstime.com:** Tommason (br); Rudmer Zwerver (b). **26 Alamy Stock Photo:** Photosargentum (tl). **Dreamstime.com:** Verastuchelova (br). **27 Alamy Stock Photo:** Blickwinkel (tr). **28 Alamy Stock Photo:** © chrisstockphotography (cl); Kim Taylor / Nature Picture Library (crb). **Dorling Kindersley:** Jerry Young (tr). **Dreamstime.com:** Shelly Still (cb). **28-29 Dreamstime.com:** Andreusk. **29 Alamy Stock Photo:** Nigel Cattlin (cla); Johner Images (fcra); Stephen Dalton / Avalon / Photoshot License (cr); Ray Wilson (fbr). **Depositphotos Inc:** VitalisG (bl). **Dreamstime.com:** DRpics24 (crb); Photographyfirm (fcr); Ilona Lablaika (fcrb). **Getty Images:** Mikroman6 (ca). **Getty Images / iStock:** NNehring (br). **naturepl.com:** Stephen Dalton (cra). **30 Alamy Stock Photo:** David Forster (cl). **Dreamstime.com:** Gorodok495 (c/Blue butterfly); Alex Petelin (tl/leaves); Jaanall (c/Wild Thyme). **Getty Images / iStock:** Antagain (cla); TellmemoreOOO (tl); Proxyminder (c). **30-31 Alamy Stock Photo:** Jim Laws (c). **Dreamstime.com:** Andrey Khokhlov; Denys Kurylow (cb); Sergii Krynytsia (cb/Ivy). **Getty Images / iStock:** Winexa (t). **31 Alamy Stock Photo:** Jim Laws (cra). **Dreamstime.com:** Antonel (c); Thorsten Nilson (cl); Alex Petelin (tr); Goldution (tr/Flower basket). **Getty Images / iStock:** Chushkin (cra/Blue Butterfly); Epantha (clb). **32 Dreamstime.com:** Banepx (c). **32-33 Dreamstime.com:** Grpstock. **Getty Images / iStock:** Tongwongboot (tc). **33 Dorling Kindersley:** Oxford University Museum of Natural History (c). **Dreamstime.com:** Chernetskaya (cr); Hecke01 (tr, ca); Wksp (br); Stargatechris (br/crumbs); Robert309 (clb). **Getty Images:** 10'000 Hours (tl). **34-35 Dreamstime.com:** Christian Schmalhofer. **36 Alamy Stock Photo:** Andrew Baskott (tr). **Dreamstime.com:** Thorsten Nilson (bc). **Getty Images / iStock:** JohnFScott (tc); Flavio Vallenari (bl). **36-37 Dreamstime.com:** Vitaly Korovin (Background). **Getty Images / iStock:** Colematt; Proxyminder (Butterfly). **37 Alamy Stock Photo:** Sylvia Buchholz / Reuters (cb). **Dreamstime.com:** Nnorozoff (cla). **Getty Images / iStock:** Charliebishop (tr). **38-39 Getty Images / iStock:** Shinytastic. **38 Alamy Stock Photo:** Dave Bevan (clb). **Dreamstime.com:** Henkbogaard (c); Mikelane45 (br). **39 Dreamstime.com:** Martin Lewis (clb). **Getty Images / iStock:** JBLumix (tl). **40 Alamy Stock Photo:** Samuel Baylis (tl); Britain - landscapes (ftl); Ernie Janes (bl). **Dreamstime.com:** Sander Meertins (cra); Mikelane45 (crb). **41 Alamy Stock Photo:** Franz Christoph Robiller / imageBROKER (tr); S C Bisserot / Nature Photographers Ltd (cr). **Depositphotos Inc:** Nicolasprimola (crb). **Dreamstime.com:** Mikelane45 (ca); Rastan (crb/sunrise). **Getty Images / iStock:** Robjem (l). **42 Alamy Stock Photo:** Zoonar / Peter Himmelhuber / Zoonar GmbH (cl); Frank Sommariva / imageBROKER (c); Marko König / imageBROKER (cb). **Dreamstime.com:** Beataaldridge (crb). **42-43 Dreamstime.com:** Chaiwat Hemakom; Roman Novitskii (b). **43 Alamy Stock Photo:** Elizabeth Bennett (tr). **Dreamstime.com:** Sander Meertins (crb); Pavel Rumlena (cr); Sgoodwin4813 (cl); Alfio Scisetti (c/mustard flowers). **Getty Images / iStock:** Andrew_Howe (cb); Paulfjs (c). **44 123RF.com:** Thomas Males (br). **Dreamstime.com:** Jmrocek (c). **Getty Images:** David Tipling / Universal Images Group (tr). **44-45 Alamy Stock Photo:** Simon Dux. **45 Alamy Stock Photo:** Frédéric Desmette / Biosphoto (tr); Buschkind (cr). **Dreamstime.com:** Christian Fogtmann (bc). **46 Alamy Stock Photo:** Laurie Campbell / Nature Photographers Ltd (br); Chris Mattison (br/Slow-worm). **Dreamstime.com:** Frank Fichtmueller (tr); Rudmer Zwerver (ca); Mihai Neacsu (clb). **46-47 Dreamstime.com:** Timonko. **47 Dreamstime.com:** Jeanninebryan (bl); Miriamstockphotos (cr). **48 Dorling Kindersley:** Natural History Museum, London (cra). **Dreamstime.com:** Stig Karlsson (crb). **48-49 Dreamstime.com:** Kirsty Pargeter. **Getty Images / iStock:** stocknshares (b). **49 123RF.com:** lanwool (tl). **Alamy Stock Photo:** Stephen Dalton / Avalon / Photoshot License (cra). **Dreamstime.com:** Ebilena69 (tr); Javier Alonso Huerta (cb); Isselee (cb/Ringlet); Mrehssani (cra/butterfly); Kristof Lauwers (br). **Getty Images / iStock:** Schnuddel (c). **50 Dreamstime.com:** Zakalinka (tr). **50-51 Dreamstime.com:** Roman Novitskii (Background). **51 Dreamstime.com:** Countrygirl1966 (br); Nataliia Yankovets (tr). **Getty Images / iStock:** Malerapaso (l). **52 Alamy Stock Photo:** John Burnham (cl); Carl Morrow (cr). **Depositphotos Inc:** Fatamorgana-999 (cb). **Dreamstime.com:** Pawel Horazy (tr); Zhanghaobeibei (crb). **53 Alamy Stock Photo:** Frank Hecker (tl); Alex Hyde / Nature Picture Library (cra); McPhoto (cl); Stefano Ravera (bl). **54 Depositphotos Inc:** Dr. Pas (br). **Dreamstime.com:** Richard Griffin (tl); Mikelane45 (clb). **55 Dreamstime.com:** Berndbrueggemann (b); Olha Rohulya (cra). **Getty Images / iStock:** ChrisHepburn (tc). **Getty Images:** David Tipling / Education Images / Universal Images Group (cl); Naturfoto Honal (cr). **56-57 Getty Images:** Arterra / Universal Images Group. **58 Dreamstime.com:** William87 (cr). **58-59 Getty Images / iStock:** fotoVoyager. **59 Dreamstime.com:** Claudiodivizia (cb); Raluca Tudor (crb). **Getty Images / iStock:** Gannet77 (tc). **Getty Images:** Arterra / Universal Images Group (cra). **60 Alamy Stock Photo:** Nick Upton / Robertharding (cb). **Dreamstime.com:** Anders93 (bc); Rudmer Zwerver (ca); Lenka Šošolíková (crb). **61 Dreamstime.com:** Anest (crb); Viter8 (tc); Pitris (ca/Buzzer midge); Isselee (c, c/Eurasian minnow); Ondřej Prosický (clb). **Getty Images / iStock:** Fabioski (cla); Ookawaphoto (ca). **62 Alamy Stock Photo:** Drew Buckley (c). **Dreamstime.com:** Orest Lyzhechka (bl). **Getty Images / iStock:** Andyworks (br). **62-63 Alamy Stock Photo:** Anna Stowe Landscapes UK. **63 Alamy Stock Photo:** Florallmages (clb); Alan Novelli (cla); Clement Philippe / Arterra Picture Library (cb). **Dreamstime.com:** Johannes Mayer (tr). **Getty Images / iStock:** Whiteway (clb/Wild mint). **64-65 Getty Images:** Gary Mayes. **64 Alamy Stock Photo:** Dummermuth Stefan / Prisma by Dukas Presseagentur GmbH (cra). **Dreamstime.com:** Mikelane45 (br). **Getty Images / iStock:** Monthian (cb). **65 Alamy Stock Photo:** Nigel Cattlin (tc). **Dreamstime.com:** Saccobent (cr); Whiskybottle (br); Slowmotiongli (cr). **66 Alamy Stock Photo:** Daniele Occhiato / Buiten-Beeld (c); Juniors Bildarchiv / F300 / Juniors Bildarchiv GmbH (tr). **Dreamstime.com:** Jaqui Taylor (b). **66-67 Alamy Stock Photo:** Arnhel de Serra / The National Trust Photolibrary. **67 Alamy Stock Photo:** Kevin Maskell (br); Geoff Smith (clb). **Dreamstime.com:** Robert Thorley (cla). **68 Alamy Stock Photo:** FLPA (cb). **Getty Images / iStock:** AlasdairJames (ca). **68-69 Dreamstime.com:** Bjorn Hovdal (t); Izanbar (b); Roman Novitskii (b/background). **69 Alamy Stock Photo:** Blickwinkel / H. Baesemann (c). **Dreamstime.com:** Mikelane45 (clb). **Science Photo Library:** Claude Nuridsany & Marie Perennou (tl). **70 Alamy Stock Photo:** Nigel Cattlin (crb); DP Wildlife Invertebrates (bl). **Dreamstime.com:** 7active Studio (br); Roman Ivaschenko (tl/Hornwort, cl, cb, crb/Hornwort); Verastuchelova (bc). **naturepl.com:** Kim Taylor (tl, ca, cla). **70-71 Dreamstime.com:** Mr.phonlawat Chaicheevinlikit. **71 Alamy Stock Photo:** Blickwinkel / Hartl (crb/snail); Christian GUY / imageBROKER (cl). **Dreamstime.com:** 7active Studio (cb); Viter8 (cra, c); Roman Ivaschenko (crb); Verastuchelova (bc); Dvoriankin (b). **Getty Images / iStock:** Sturti (tr). **72-73 Dreamstime.com:** Sabellopro. **72 Alamy Stock Photo:** Rex May (bc). **Dreamstime.com:** Anna Barwick (tl); Dubults (cr). **73 Dreamstime.com:** Ildiko Laskay (cra); Sander Meertins (cr); Dawn Quadling (cl); Nitsuki (cb). **74-75 Alamy Stock Photo:** Clement Philippe / Arterra Picture Library. **76 Alamy Stock Photo:** Ernie Janes (tr). **Dreamstime.com:** Rudmer Zwerver (cb); Richard Sriskandan (bl). **Dreamstime.com:** David Head (cl). **Getty Images:** Tajinder Singh Thiara / EyeEm (cb). **76-77 Alamy Stock Photo:** Stephen Davies. **77 Alamy Stock Photo:** Keith Morris News (tr). **Dreamstime.com:** Philip Bird (bl). **Getty Images:** Tim Graham (ca). **78-79 Dreamstime.com:** Howard Brown; Roman Novitskii (b). **78 Alamy Stock Photo:** Fergus Gill / Nature Picture Library (c). **79 123RF.com:** Michael Lane (c); Michael Mill (bc). **Dreamstime.com:** Toni Genes (cl). **80 Alamy Stock Photo:** Sabena Jane Blackbird (c). **Getty Images / iStock:** Arnaud Abadie (cl). **80-81 Alamy Stock Photo:** Steve Taylor ARPS (c); Magdalena Kvarning; David Brabiner (Background). **Dreamstime.com:** Roman Novitskii (b). **81 Alamy Stock Photo:** Philip Bird (c). **82 123RF.com:** Vitalii Gulay / Vitalisg (tr). **Alamy Stock Photo:** Frank Hecker (c). **82-83 Dreamstime.com:** Tottoto. **83 Alamy Stock Photo:** Adam Burton (tl). **Depositphotos Inc:** Getino13 (c). **Dreamstime.com:** Henrikhl (b). **84 Depositphotos Inc:** Vitor (crb). **Dreamstime.com:** Ollyhitchen01 (cra). **Getty Images / iStock:** Mauribo (cl). **84-85 Alamy Stock Photo:** James Osmond. **85 Alamy Stock Photo:** Nature Picture Library (cr). **Dreamstime.com:** Blanscape (fcr); Sander Meertins (ca); Anahita Daklani (cl); Tetiana Kovalenko (cra); Rudmer Zwerver (bl). **Getty Images / iStock:** Dapec (tr). **86-87 Getty Images / iStock:** Whitemay. **86 Alamy Stock Photo:** Arco / G. Lacz / Imagebroker (cb); Ian Redding (ca). **Getty Images / iStock:** Mauribo (tr). **naturepl.com:** Ingo Arndt (crb). **87 Alamy Stock Photo:** Paul R. Sterry / Nature Photographers Ltd (ca). **Dreamstime.com:** Denis Kelly / Deniskelly (crb), Chris Dorney (ca/Dwyryd Estuary), Loflo69 (clb), David Watson (bc). **88 Alamy Stock Photo:** Marcus McAdam (tl). **Dorling Kindersley:** National Birds of Prey Centre, Gloucestershire (br). **88-89 Dreamstime.com:** Agami Photo Agency (c); Michael Valos. **89 123RF.com:** Eric Isselee (bl). **Alamy Stock Photo:** digitalunderwater.com (cr); Nature Picture Library (crb). **Dreamstime.com:** Izanbar (cl). **90-91 Getty Images:** Morgan Stephenson. **92 Alamy Stock Photo:** SEUK News (cra). **Getty Images / iStock:** Paul Carpenter (clb). **92-93 Dreamstime.com:** Rehanali1711. **93 Alamy Stock Photo:** Kathy deWitt (tr). **Getty Images:** Chandan Khanna / AFP (ca). **94 123RF.com:** Maksym Bondarchuk (cr). **Dreamstime.com:** Ekaterina Arkhangelskaia (fcr); Bugtiger (fcr/Azalea flowers); Zerbor (br). **95 Alamy Stock Photo:** Frank Teigler / Premium Stock Photography GmbH (c). **Dreamstime.com:** Jaroslav Kettner (tc); Robert Kneschke (tl); Aleksandr Proshkin (tr); Denys Kurylow (bl). **96 Dreamstime.com:** Monika Adamczyk (fbr); Lubos Chlubny (br); Valentyn75 (br/Acorn). **Getty Images / iStock:** Andyworks (cra); Stefonlinton (c). **Shutterstock.com:** FLPA (cla). **96-97 Alamy Stock Photo:** Graham Prentice. **Dreamstime.com:** Farmer (bc); Vvoevale (c). **97 Alamy Stock Photo:** Andrew Darrington (c); Colin Varndell (bl). **Dreamstime.com:** Sataporn Jiwjalaen / Onairjiw (r). **Shutterstock.com:** Nielsdk / imageBROKER (bc). **98-99 Dreamstime.com:** Yordan Rusev (bc); TonyTaylorStock. **Getty Images / iStock:** Simonbradfield (Background). **98 Alamy Stock Photo:** Chris Mattison / Nature Picture Library (cr). **Dreamstime.com:** Yordan Rusev (crb); Shaunwilkinson (ca); Rudmer Zwerver (cb). **99 Alamy Stock Photo:** Alan Keith Beastall (clb); Clement Philippe / Arterra Picture Library (br). **Dreamstime.com:** Jmrocek (tc); Tomasztc (bl); Julia Sudnitskaya (cr). **100 Alamy Stock Photo:** Justus de Cuveland / imageBROKER (cra); Colin Varndell (cb). **Dreamstime.com:** Thomas Lukassek (cl); Osipovfoto (crb). **100-101 Dreamstime.com:** Loeskieboom (Background); Sandra Standbridge (cb). **Getty Images:** Luthfy Prayoga / EyeEm (b). **101 Alamy Stock Photo:** Andrew Darrington (cla); David J. Green (cl). **102 Alamy Stock Photo:** Tim Graham (cra). **Dreamstime.com:** Harald Biebel (b). **102-103 Alamy Stock Photo:** Craig Joiner Photography (bc); David Noton Photography. **103 Alamy Stock Photo:** Papilio (cr). **Dreamstime.com:** Alexander Hasenkampf (crb); Emma Ros (bc); Photographieundmehr (clb); Whiskybottle (br). **104-105 Alamy Stock Photo:** Kevin Prönnecke / imageBROKER. **104 Dreamstime.com:** Karl Ander Adami (tr); Michal Pešata (tl). **Getty Images / iStock:** Ugniz (b). **105 123RF.com:** Piotr Krześlak (tl). **Alamy Stock Photo:** Blickwinkel / K. Wothe (cb); Mike Lane (cl). **Dreamstime.com:** Slowmotiongli (cra); Svehlik21 (bl). **Getty Images:** Wilhelm Linse (br). **106 Alamy Stock Photo:** Adrian Davies (ca). **Dreamstime.com:** Vladyslav Siaber (cb); Vitalssss (cr). **107 Alamy Stock Photo:** Neil Hardwick (ca). **Dreamstime.com:** Vitalinar (cla). **108 Alamy Stock Photo:** Henry Ausloos (crb); Clement Philippe / Arterra Picture Library (cb). Dreamstime.com: Dennis Jacobsen (c); Silviu Matei (cra). **108-109 Alamy Stock Photo:** André Gilden. **109 Alamy Stock Photo:** Mick Durham FRPS (clb); Markus Varesvuo / Nature Picture Library (cla); Wild Wonders of Europe / Widstrand / Nature Picture Library (tr). **Dreamstime.com:** Geoffrey Kuchera (br). **110-111 Getty Images / iStock:** technotr. **112 Getty Images / iStock:** Halbergman (tc). **112-113 Dreamstime.com:** Frizzantine. **113 Alamy Stock Photo:** Julie Fryer Images (crb); Wiert Nieuman (ca). **Getty Images / iStock:** Steve Adams (tl); FotoVoyager (cb). **114-115 Getty Images / iStock:** Mauinow1. **114 Depositphotos Inc:** Paolo-Manzi (crb). **Dreamstime.com:** Jmrocek (bl). **115 Alamy Stock Photo:** Franz Christoph Robiller / imageBROKER (ca). **Dreamstime.com:** Roman Novitskii (r). **Getty Images / iStock:** CreativeNature_nl (cb). **116 Alamy Stock Photo:** Jerome Murray - CC (tr); Tony Mills (cl). **Dreamstime.com:** Andreevaee (fcl); Ian Redding (cr). **116-117 Dreamstime.com:** Minnystock. **117 Alamy Stock Photo:** Reinhard Hölzl / imageBROKER (c); Bernd Zoller / imageBROKER (cr); Paroli Galperti / REDA &CO srl (bl). **Dreamstime.com:** Agami Photo Agency (tl); Phartisan (c/Rock). **Getty Images:** Arterra / Universal Images Group (br). **Getty Images / iStock:** Dirk Strothmann (br/rocks). **118 Dreamstime.com:** Ondřej Prosický (cl). **Getty Images / iStock:** Tadas_Zvinklys (cla). **118-119 Dreamstime.com:** Halina Koktysh; Ondřej Prosický (ca). **119 Dreamstime.com:** Cowboy54 (cb); Дмитрий Михайлюк (clb); Sakalouski Uladzislau (br); Max5128 (crb). **120-121 Alamy Stock Photo:** MediaWorldImages (cl). **120 Alamy Stock Photo:** Clement Philippe / Arterra Picture Library (c/Alpine); MediaWorldImages (c/Scottish moorland); Mark Hamblin / 2020VISION / Nature Picture Library (bc). **121 Alamy Stock Photo:** MediaWorldImages (cl); Giedrius Stakauskas (bl); Gordon Mills (b); Andrea Innocenti / REDA &CO srl (br). **Dreamstime.com:** Samuel Areny (cr). **Shutterstock.com:** Bob Gibbons / Flpa / imageBROKER (cl). **122 123RF.com:** Dolgachov (clb). **Alamy Stock Photo:** Bob Gibbons (cl); Roar Loven (bl); Blickwinkel / Hecker (cr). **Dreamstime.com:** Belizar (crb); Iakov Filimonov (cla); Roman Ivaschenko (cb). **123 Alamy Stock Photo:** FLPA (tl); Manfred Ruckszio (cra, c); Arndt Sven-Erik / Arterra Picture Library (br). **Dreamstime.com:** Mikelane45 (crb); Petrsalinger (bl). **124 Dreamstime.com:** LittleAdventures (tc). **125 123RF.com:** Michael Lane (cr); Michael Mill (br). **128 Getty Images / iStock:** Ookawaphoto (tl)
**Cover images:** *Front:* **123RF.com:** Andrzej Tokarski / ajt ca/ (snail); **Alamy Stock Photo:** Richard Becker clb, Paul Mayall Birds cb, Prisma by Dukas Presseagentur GmbH crb; **Depositphotos Inc:** jee1999 ca; **Dreamstime.com:** Chernetskaya, Coatsey Coatsey b; **Getty Images / iStock:** Malerapaso cra; *Back:* **123RF.com:** Andrzej Tokarski / ajt ca/ (snail), Lillian Tveit crb; **Depositphotos Inc:** jee1999 ca; **Dreamstime.com:** Chernetskaya, Coatsey Coatsey tl, Countrygirl1966 bl, Fosterss cla; **Getty Images / iStock:** Malerapaso cra, fbl; *Spine:* **123RF.com:** Andrzej Tokarski / ajt ca/ (snail); **Depositphotos Inc:** jee1999 ca

All other images © Dorling Kindersley
For further information see: www.dkimages.com